MEDITATIONS
On *the*
Mysteries
Of the
Rosary

Kenneth R. Wichorek

MEDITATIONS on the MYSTERIES of the ROSARY
by Kenneth R. Wichorek

Printed in the United States of America

ISBN 9781622304172

Unless otherwise indicated, Bible quotations are taken from The Holy Bible; The Catholic Bible; and The Douay-Rheims Version. Copyright © 1941 by Benziger Brothers, Inc.

Other Books by Wichorek
Suffering Christ on the Cross
Our Third Life

This book was written with the official teachings of the Catholic Church in mind. The author willingly submits himself to the ultimate official pronouncement of the Catholic Church on any of the content of this book.

www.xulonpress.com

This book is dedicated to the Blessed Virgin Mary

Acknowledgments

I wish to express my thanks and appreciation to my wife Rita for her help in editing this book and for her support and patience. My faith would not have been possible without the teaching, prayers, and help I have received by so very many priests and religious throughout the years.

CONTENTS

THE GIFT OF LOVE

By Kenneth R. Wichorek

The warm sun above, the sky so blue,
    The cool breeze blows, there is so much to do,
Walking, hiking, swimming, fishing so cool,
    and food so delicious it makes one drool.
Oh! What a wonderful Gift of Life, even for a fool.
A seed if dropped into the ground,
    water flows to the seed all around.
The sun upon rising spreads its light,
    then the seed to its delight,
Begins to form its Gift of Life.
A salmon against the water fights,
    and swims with all its might,
till at last it stops to rest
    among the stones and currents to nest;
then the eggs to her delight,
    begins to form its Gift of Life.
Above the mighty trees, the eagle soars and sees,
    a worthy place to which to flee;
she rests and then her eggs she lays,

a marvel that we all can say,
It's a Gift of Life today.
The moose across the meadow goes,
across the stream where water flows;
To bring forth from her place,
a little one to kick her face,
A Gift of Life born without haste.
The greatest gift I must confess,
though these births are great, not less,
is the woman who would bring
a lovely baby that all could sing;
a Gift of Life, let the bells ring!
Lives there a person so cruel and cold,
who would not acknowledge when told,
a baby girl or boy will be born?
Guard this life does God not warn?
Rejoice! The greatest Gift of Life, sound the horn!

PREFACE

While Jesus prayed frequently to his Father, his prayers can only be understood as his humanity praying on behalf of all humanity as well as his human self. Since God the Father has given over to Jesus the task of saving humanity, all prayer is really channeled through Jesus to God even though Jesus is one of the members of the Trinity. The sacrifice of Jesus has produced an infinite treasure of grace which can be used by our prayers when in conformity to the will of God. Prayer to the Blessed Virgin Mary is no different than when we ask someone to pray for us except that she is in heaven and is close to God. That this prayer is pleasing to God is demonstrated by the many favors and miracles granted by those prayers.

In the beginning the early monks and clergy prayed the 150 Psalms that are in the Bible. Since the laity could not read, they said the Our Father instead. The practice grew of people keeping track of how many they said by using stones and later a string of knots or beads. Some people said the Hail Mary instead of the Our Father.

Tradition tells us that while St. Dominic was praying and doing penance for three days and nights for help in converting the Albigensians, the Blessed Virgin Mary appeared to him. She wanted the Psalter said with 150 Hail Marys, a prayer that was to become the Rosary. She divided it into 15 parts in order to recall and picture the events in the life of Jesus. So now everyone could picture the life of Jesus no matter what his level of education was. Eventually other prayers were added to complete the rosary as it's prayed today.

We should look at the rosary as a journey to God through Jesus with the eyes of Mary. The mysteries are taken mostly from the Bible and arranged in a somewhat logical order. One should keep in mind the general theme of the mystery.

As one prays the rosary, that person should meditate on the mystery of that decade of the rosary, Many times this is difficult to do as we are so easily distracted and the ten Hail Marys go by so quickly. Also, it is not so easy for many of us to reach this level of meditation. It is with this thought in mind that this book is written. These meditations are not intended to be said prior to reciting the rosary itself, but are rather intended for a quiet meditation on only one particular mystery. I hope to provide a greater insight into each particular mystery and of course you are encouraged to expand on what I have offered. The Blessed Virgin Mary at Fatima promised special graces at the hour of death for all those who on the first Saturday of five consecutive months: 1. Goes to Confession and receives Communion, 2. Recites five decades of the Rosary, and 3. Keeps her company for 15 minutes by meditating on the Mysteries of the Rosary with the intention of making reparation to her Immaculate Heart. These meditations can be used to satisfy the requirement for meditating on the Rosary Mysteries.

INTRODUCTION

*G*ENERAL: The Rosary Mysteries have been somewhat expanded in chronology so as to tell a more complete story of Jesus and Mary. I have used the chronology given by Anna Catharina Emmerick's visions related in the Books The Life of Christ. While you may not agree with the chronology, a careful examination of the Biblical accounts of the events is not contradicted by this chronology. The Gospel accounts are for the most part not concerned with historical accuracy but with the meaning of the events.

THE JOYFUL MYSTERIES: These five mysteries begin the story of our redemption by Jesus through the eyes of the Blessed Virgin Mary. It begins with the incarnation of Jesus through the workings of the Holy Spirit in Nazareth. Then we are led to Mary's visit to her cousin Elizabeth who is soon to give birth to John the Baptist. From there we are led to the birth of Jesus in Bethlehem in an animal's cave. The following mystery takes up the presentation of Jesus in the Temple in Jerusalem where some extraordinary prophecies are made. The last mystery is the finding of Jesus in the Jerusalem Temple. All these events may be found in the New Testament of the Bible. Our meditation will not only be on the central event but also on other events taking place as a result of that event or those occurring after the central event. It is hoped the reader will be led to the joy experienced by Mary through the event being meditated on. However there will be a thread of sorrow running through most of these mysteries which will not be forgotten. The first sorrows of Mary and also of Saint Joseph take place during these Joyful mysteries.

THE LUMINOUS MYSTERIES: This recent addition to the Rosary takes up the life of Jesus during the three years of his preaching mission. These Mysteries are composed of two parts. First is the knowledge that Jesus really is God, Himself, the second Person of the Blessed Trinity. This knowledge is lost on everyone even the followers of Jesus. Second is the knowledge that the mission of the Messiah, Jesus, is to redeem the human race and bring people into a heavenly kingdom. This teaching also was missed by everyone as they were all looking for an earthly kingdom like that of King David. Jesus starts his mission by being anointed by the Holy Spirit which takes place when he is baptized by John the Baptist. Jesus shows his miraculous power by changing water into wine at a wedding feast where his Apostles become acquainted with Jesus, his relatives, and each other. Then Jesus spends the three years preaching to the crowds and working many miracles. The transfiguration of Jesus takes place in the presence of three Apostles where he shows his glorified body and he converses with Moses and Elijah. He demonstrates that he is the Messiah. The last Mystery is at the Last Supper where Jesus changes bread and wine into his Body and Blood and gives this power as a gift to his Church in the following centuries.

THE SORROWFUL MYSTERIES: These mysteries take place after the Last Supper and are the beginning of the Passion and Death of Jesus Christ. It begins in the garden of Gethsemani where Jesus beholds the reason for his Passion, all the sins of the human race, the sufferings he will undergo, and the results of his actions. His sufferings are so terrible that Jesus sweats blood. The second mystery recalls the terrible scourging of Jesus followed by the crowning of thorns by the soldiers. The agonizing slow journey of Jesus to Calvary is the fourth meditation. This is followed by the last meditation, the crucifixion and death of Jesus on the wooden cross.

THE GLORIOUS MYSTERIES: These mysteries complete the Rosary. The first mystery is the resurrection of Jesus from the dead. The disbelief recounted by the disciples of Jesus is echoed by many persons today. This mystery is followed by the ascension of Jesus who joins his heavenly Father in heaven. The third mystery is the descent of the Holy Spirit on the Apostles who are inflamed with courage and boldly proclaim the good news to the world. The last two mysteries concern Mary. While the Assumption and Coronation of Mary is not mentioned in the Bible, it can be inferred in its writings. These two mysteries have been believed by Christians since the earliest times and are mentioned in many early Christian writings.

ANNUNCIATION

*A*nd in the sixth month, the angel Gabriel was sent
*from God into a city of Galilee, called Nazareth,
To a virgin espoused to a man whose name was Joseph,
of the house of David: and the virgin's name was Mary.
And the angel being come in, said unto her: Hail, full
of grace, the Lord is with thee: blessed art thou among
women. Who having heard, was troubled at his saying
and thought with herself what manner of salutation this
should be. And the angel said to her: Fear not, Mary,
for thou hast found grace with God. Behold thou shalt
conceive in thy womb and shalt bring forth a son: and
thou shalt call his name Jesus. He shall be great and
shall be called the Son of the Most High. And the Lord
God shall give unto him the throne of David his father:
and he shall reign in the house of Jacob forever. And of
his kingdom there shall be no end. And Mary said to the
angel: How shall this be done, because I know not man?
And the angel answering, said to her: The Holy Ghost
shall come upon thee and the power of the Most High
shall overshadow thee. And therefore also the Holy which
shall be born of thee shall be called the Son of God. And*

behold thy cousin Elizabeth, she also hath conceived a son in her old age: and this is the sixth month with her that is called barren. Because no word shall be impossible with God. And Mary said: Behold the handmaid of the Lord: be it done to me according to thy word. And the angel departed from her. (LK 1:26-38)

Our story really goes back in time to the beginning of creation when Adam and Eve lived in perfect harmony with God. In sinning against God, their supernatural gifts were taken away from them, life took on burdens and sufferings, and would end in death. This is what all the descendants of Adam and Eve inherited. But God made a promise that some day a woman's descendant will triumph. And this is what this meditation is all about. Mary is the new Eve. Eve was created immaculate with a rib taken from Adam. Mary was conceived immaculate, that is free from original sin. So, she is rightfully called the Immaculate Conception, a title she gave herself at Lourdes France to a little girl, St. Bernadette. Mary was given this great gift in recognition of her future perfect obedience to the will of God. One tradition is that Mary, about 3 years old, entered the temple at Jerusalem where she grew in devotion and love of God. Thus, one can see in Mary a true and perfect tabernacle for God to enter. Humanly speaking, it is impossible for any member of the human race to make restitution to God for any offense against God. Humans are creatures of God who is Himself uncreated and lacks nothing. While God is not harmed by sin, sin causes tremendous disorder to mankind as one can see from the actions of humans throughout the centuries. The most intelligent philosopher would have to conclude that reconciliation with God is impossible. God is perfect and lacks nothing. Man, on the other hand, owes everything especially his existence to God. However, all things are possible with God and God has found a solution, a proper punishment for mankind and a way for man to regain his original friendship with God. From the earliest times, man had been searching for God and attempting to bring God into a close relationship with himself. Man's efforts were revolting in contrast to the true nature of God. Heavenly bodies, animals, and even men were proclaimed gods and were worshiped. The true beauty that God intended for humans was grotesquely twisted. Finally God, through Abraham and Moses, had to reeducate a select group of humans to the true nature of God. God gave them commandments and rules to govern their lives. When they went astray and sinned, God sent prophets to attempt to correct them, It was these prophets who foretold the coming of the Messiah who would fulfill the promise originally made to Adam and Eve. Sadly, this Messiah, the Anointed One of God, began to be thought of as an earthly king who would restore an earthly kingdom to the Jewish nation. This was the situation at the time of Mary when there was a great expectation of the coming of the Messiah. Everyone thought this Messiah would restore the kingdom of David and throw out the Roman conquerors. While idol worship in Judaea had been eliminated by the Jews, the religion handed on by Moses had become wrapped up in minute regulations far from the spirit of Judaism. Mary, deep in prayer, prayed for the coming of the Messiah. She begged that she would be chosen to serve the Messiah's mother as her handmaid. So humble was Mary that there was no thought on her part that she could be the mother of the Messiah. She felt herself so unworthy that the thought never even entered her mind. Let us consider this scene to see what we can learn from Mary. Mary is praying deeply for God's promise of a Messiah to be accomplished. In other words that God's will be done. She does this by acknowledging her own unworthiness with humility. Her whole focus is on what God wants to do and there is no thought about herself except how she could help the Messiah's mother. This is the way we need to approach prayer to God with humility. There should be no thought of ourself except how we can help the accomplishment of God's will. Just as Mary learned about God in the Temple, we need to learn about God's ways from the Church. Mary spent ten years praying and listening to God's word. We certainly need to spend a great deal of time learning our faith. This is best done by listening to the teachings of the Church which Jesus gave us to ensure that we stay on the straight and narrow path. There are many ways to do this. We should listen attentively to the readings and sermons at Mass. We should read and if necessary study the catechism of the Catholic Church. Armed with this information we are then better able to pray to God. We can then better focus on what God wants and not so much on what we want. Mary's prayer was humble. Our prayer must be humble as we should recognize that we are praying to God who is so far above any human being and that we have been so unfaithful to God in the past. Yet, we know that no matter how unworthy we are, God will listen to our prayer and he will always answer us. Our prayer should always end as Mary's did with God's will in mind. The angel's initial greeting tells us a great deal about Mary. The angel says that she is "full of grace". Who of us can honestly say that we are full of grace. In order to be full of grace we would need to be completely void of any sin. Mary is full of grace not only because there was no stain of original sin from Adam and Eve in her, but also because she was herself sinless. We now know that she remained sinless throughout her entire life. This fact alone should arouse our admiration and love for her. Mary can be a great help to us in our quest to remain faithful and obedient to God. The next revelation about Mary that we hear from the angel is that "the Lord is with you". Who of us would not want to hear these words spoken about us. It is in studying Mary that we can get closer to God and someday recognize that God is with us.. Mary's primary role with us is to help us to know, love, and remain faithful to God so that after this life is over we can join Him in heaven. It is understandable that Mary is troubled by the angel's initial greeting as anyone of us would be. "Fear not," the angel says, "you have found grace with God". Mary was troubled but the angel told her not to be afraid. We too become afraid of certain events in our life and like Mary we should not be afraid. We just need to call on God for assistance and we know that God is always faithful and he will help us even if we have let him down. The angel delivers the message he was sent to deliver. Mary's reaction is certainly different from what our reaction would be. Mary showed a great deal of trust and fidelity to God's purpose which was the central point of the message, the birth of the Messiah. She questioned how she could accomplish it as "I know not man". Mary had consecrated herself to God and to have relations with Joseph would have broken her vow. Mary did not question what God wanted to accomplish, instead she wanted to know how she could accomplish this since she assumed that God did not want her to break her vow of virginity. The angel then provides the answer to the only question that Mary had regarding the angel's message. The Holy Spirit of God would overshadow Mary so that she could conceive a child. A son who would be called the Son of God. She is told to name him Jesus. A name which means God saves. We see here the action of the Holy Trinity. God the Father sends the Word of God, his Son, through the power of the Holy Spirit. The angel gives Mary another piece of information. Her cousin Elizabeth who was an old woman and childless was pregnant in her sixth month. The angel, to add emphasis to his message, tells Mary that nothing is impossible with God. Many times we seem to suggest by our actions that God can't do something. Yet we know better. There is nothing that is impossible for God. The problem is that we are not trustful enough or else what we want is not in consonant with God's will. We need to remind ourselves of this message that the angel delivered to Mary. There is nothing impossible for God. The angel waited and did not leave after he delivered his message. This is unusual as the angel messengers always leave after the message is delivered. There must be something more. The angel is waiting for Mary's consent. Just think. If Mary had said no thanks, then who knows what would have transpired in history. But God had picked the right person. Mary's answer was that she was only a servant and that she would do what God wanted according to the angel's message.. What great humility was shown by Mary at this moment. Remember, she was going to be the mother of the Messiah and God was going to accomplish this through the Holy Spirit. Her son would be called the Son of God. This meditation is about Mary and God. Mary's role in our life is to lead us to God. God came to her in the Incarnation. Mary's great love for God followed by her attentive learning about God and her long hours in prayer resulted in Mary mastering humility. We cannot approach God unless we cultivate this virtue of humility. Mary, the new Eve, perfectly obeyed God even when she did not completely understand the message of God.. She cannot replace Eve as our earthly mother, but she can as our spiritual mother. Mary's obedience was founded on her complete trust in God. We do well to imitate Mary's love. At long last, God the Father puts his plan to restore mankind to his friendship by sending his Son to become human just like us in all things except sin. Jesus will offer up to God as an equal the necessary ransom on behalf of mankind to not only free us from sin and Satan but to open the door for an everlasting relationship with God in heaven.

VISITATION

*A*nd Mary rising up in those days, went into the hill country with haste into a city of Juda. And she entered into the house of Zachary and saluted Elizabeth. And it came to pass that when Elizabeth heard the salutation of Mary, the infant leaped in her womb. And Elizabeth was filled with the Holy Ghost. And she cried out with a loud voice and said: Blessed art thou among women and blessed is the fruit of thy womb. And whence is this to me that the mother of my Lord should come to me? For behold as soon as the voice of thy salutation sounded in my ears, the infant in my womb leaped for joy. And blessed art thou that hast believed, because those things shall be accomplished that were spoken to thee by the Lord. And Mary said: My soul doth magnify the Lord. And my spirit hath rejoiced in God my Saviour. Because he hath regarded the humility of his handmaid: for behold from henceforth all generations shall call me blessed. Because he that is mighty hath done great things to me: and holy is his name. And his mercy is from generation unto generations, to them that fear him. He hath shewed might in his arm: he hath scattered the proud in *the conceit of their heart. He hath put down the mighty from their seat and hath exalted the humble. He hath filled the hungry with good things: and the rich he hath sent empty away. He hath received Israel his servant, being mindful of his mercy. As he spoke to our fathers: to Abraham and to his seed for ever. And Mary abode with her about three months. And she returned to her own house.* (LK1:39-56)

After the conception of Jesus, Mary had a great desire to visit her cousin Elizabeth. So, seated on a donkey, she set out with Joseph on the long journey to Zachary's house. This joy of Mary bearing the barely infant Jesus is the same joy which we should experience when we are carrying the resurrected Jesus in our bodies after Holy Communion. Joseph undoubtedly held back as Mary ran into the house to greet Elizabeth. Elizabeth for her part must have received some knowledge in a vision about the Messiah's birth. The infant in Elizabeth's womb leaped with joy at Mary's greeting. A sign that the Holy Spirit had removed original sin from the future St. John the Baptist. So that later Jesus could say that of all men born of women, John the Baptist was the greatest. And in her humility, Elizabeth questioned why the mother of the Messiah was visiting her. Elizabeth blesses Mary because she believed and did not question the request of God. Mary's great faith and obedience overshadows the faith and obedience of everyone who proceeded her. Unlike Eve who planted the seed of disobedience in mankind, Mary accepted the seed of obedience, God, Himself. Mary, the Immaculate Conception, was to give each of us the means to a rebirth through her son, Jesus. Mary glorifies God because he has done great things for her and all generations will call her blessed. While Mary may be thinking about being the mother of the Messiah when she said these words, they would become true in a greater sense as Mary would go on to not only remain sinless but to join Jesus in the sufferings of his passion. Mary continues praising God echoing the words of Old Testament women. We are not told anything more about Mary's visit except that she stayed three months. We can only conjecture what Mary and Elizabeth talked about and it is probable that Mary was there when the birth of John the Baptist took place. Two women of great faith and love for God would have spent their time praying and discussing what the future would be for their two sons. Both women familiar with the scriptures would undoubtedly have discussed the roles of the Messiah and the forerunner of the Messiah as they both understood the roles of their children. Unaware of the sufferings to come, their time would have been joyful. We could do well to follow the example of these two women and face our future with joy and prayer. We must be mindful that whatever the future holds for us, it is what the will of God allows. So our will must unite itself to God's will, willingly and cheerfully. Elizabeth's child was born and eight days later when he was to be circumcised, they called him Zachary, his father's name. But his mother said no, his name is John. His father, Zachary, then wrote on a tablet, as he still could not speak as he had doubted the angel's previous message to him, his name is John. Then Zachary filled with the Holy Spirit uttered these words: *"Blessed be the Lord God of Israel: because he hath visited and wrought the redemption of his people. And hath raised up an horn of salvation to us, in the house of David his servant. As he spoke by the mouth of his holy prophets, who are from the beginning. Salvation from our enemies and from the hand of all that hate us. To perform mercy to our fathers and to remember his holy testament. The oath, which he swore to Abraham our father, that he would grant to us. That being delivered from the hand of our enemies, we may serve him without fear: In holiness and justice before him, all our days. And thou, child, shalt be called the prophet of the Highest: for thou shalt go before the face of the Lord to prepare his ways: To give knowledge of salvation to his people, unto the remission of their sins. Through the bowels of the mercy of our God, in which the Orient from on high hath visited us: To enlighten them that sit in darkness and in the shadow of death: to direct our feet into the way of peace." (LK 1:68-79)* Unlike Mary, Zachary doubted the angel's message. After all his wife was old and past the age of childbearing, he wanted further proof. He was given it by being struck dumb until he fulfilled the angel's word by writing John on the tablet. Sometimes like Zachary, we find it hard to accept some of the teachings of Jesus and his Church. Instead of talking too much, we could emulate the example given to Zachary and remain silent and listen in quiet contemplation. The message of Zachary can be divided into two distinct parts. The first part talks about the coming of the Messiah and the second part proclaims John as his prophet who will prepare the way for the Messiah. At the beginning, God is blessed and thanked for giving a Messiah to Israel. It is taken for granted that this event is going to happen. It is a sure thing. It is going to happen just as the prophets foretold, a foregone conclusion. What this is to mean is salvation from their enemies and freedom. Now, those listening felt that this meant freedom from the occupation of the Romans. Surely the Messiah will be like the great king David who conquered all his enemies. Very few people realized that this freedom would be a spiritual freedom from the devil. Mary and Elizabeth, inspired by the Holy Spirit, may have realized this, but not the others. How can God be served without fear in holiness and justice under a foreign pagan government? The answer will come when Jesus appears and tells us about the kingdom of heaven, the kingdom of God. The second part of Zachary's message tells us that John is to be the prophet of the Highest. This tells us that John is to be a prophet of God and there is more. John is to go before the face of the Lord to prepare his ways. In other words, John is a great prophet who will prepare the people for the coming of the great Messiah. His mission is to show the people how to be saved. For the one who comes will show the people how to have their sins erased. John is to be the one who will not only prepare the people for the coming of this great Messiah, but he will be the one to point him out to the people. The last part of this message tells us a great deal about what this Messiah will do. He will light the way to true knowledge of God because the people are in darkness. In other words, they just don't truly know the ways of God. But now God in his great mercy will enlighten them because of his great mercy. He will guide and lead them into the way of peace. Today we can look at these words and realize their true and full meaning. Jesus, the face of God, came not only to teach us about God, not only to take away our sins, but to completely redeem us so that we are once more capable of entering heaven as was God's original intention with Adam and Eve. To do this we need to be enlightened by Jesus about the life God has intended for us. This is a life of peace in our souls once we accept Jesus and follow his commandments. We know now that this does not mean a life of ease here on earth now, but a peaceful life after our death, of everlasting happiness with God in the new world he will create at the end of this world. Many people in the world today are living in the same darkness that Zachary talks about. They are swept up in marvels and attractions of the present day world. Everyone seems to seek their own personal gratification whether it be sex, power, or money. Yet, this does not bring about true happiness. This strong pull toward personal gratification can only be stopped by prayer. Mary through her personal prayer for the coming of the Messiah realized it in a greater manner than she could ever have imagined. Elizabeth received the blessing of having a child even after she was beyond the age of childbearing. Zachary learned a great lesson when he disbelieved the great news the angel gave him. He was made mute, unable to speak for more than nine months, until he fulfilled the angel's prophecy by naming the child John. In solitude he had plenty of time to pray and think about the word of God spoken by the angel. As time marches on we see all about us a darkness that refuses to go away. The wreckage of nations, the sufferings of the poor and wounded, and the immorality of the well to do. It would appear that God has abandoned us. Rather it is because God has given us the greatest gift anyone could have, the gift of doing anything we want. A gift that is true freedom when used for good. There is in this world a shining light seen and acknowledged by only a few: The light of God's church that Jesus founded with Peter and the Apostles. We can see here the beginning of the completion of the promises that God made to Moses, Elijah, and all the Old Testament prophets. John, who would be called the Baptist, would be the last one and the only one to see the promised Messiah. A Messiah unlike the one that everyone at that time expected. Instead, He would be greater for He is God, Himself. He would prove to be the Messiah by fulfilling all the prophecies of the Old Testament and prove Himself to be God by rising from the dead. His death was seen and acknowledged by both Romans and Jews. His life after death was seen by thousands of witnesses. In this mystery, we learned about the loving compassion Mary had for her cousin Elizabeth. Zachary reveals to us that even when we disbelieve God, he will find a means to awaken our faith as he did by making Zachary mute. The birth of John the Baptist led to the eventual coming of Jesus. With our prayers and the help of Mary and the saints, we too can experience the coming of Jesus into our hearts.

NATIVITY

A *nd Joseph also went up from Galilee, out of the city of Nazareth, into Judea, to the city of David, which is called Bethlehem: because he was of the house and family of David. To be enrolled with Mary his espoused wife, who was with child. And it came to pass that when they were there, her days were accomplished that she should be delivered. And she brought forth her first-born son and wrapped him up in swaddling clothes and laid him in a manger: because there was no room for them in the inn. And there were in the same country shepherds watching and keeping the night watches over their flock. And behold an angel of the Lord stood by them and the brightness of God shone round about them: and they feared with a great fear. And the angel said to them: Fear not; for, behold, I bring you good tidings of great joy that shall be to all the people: For, this day is born to you a Saviour, who is Christ the Lord, in the city of David. And this shall be a sign unto you. You shall find the infant wrapped in swaddling clothes and laid in a manger. And suddenly there was with the angel a multitude of the heavenly army, praising God and saying: Glory to God*

*in the highest: and on earth peace to men of good will.
(LK 2: 4-14)*

The birth of a King's son or an Emperor's son was usually celebrated by cannon blasts, fireworks, and shouts of joy. Proclamations were made to the people and there would be feasting and many celebrations throughout the land. Everyone, even in far-off lands, would be aware of the birth of the King's son. Why then did the birth of God's Son take place in a remote Roman outpost in the outskirts of an insignificant town of Bethlehem in a cave used by animals? God's ways are not our ways. It is easy to see that God had to show that He had come to redeem all mankind not the rich or powerful. Also, God needed to show that He was not only aware of our trials and sufferings, but that He had also experienced them first hand even to being born just as we are. So, the birth of Jesus was announced by angels only to humble shepherds while they watched their flocks of sheep. Mary and Joseph welcomed the shepherds who came to see the newborn Jesus. The story of the shepherds undoubtedly resulted in visits by neighboring men and women. There would be nothing extraordinary about this newborn infant except for the stories of the angel's announcement. Consider now what Mary had to go through. While nine months pregnant, she traveled many miles on a donkey, which surely is not a comfortable mode of travel, to the town of Bethlehem where she found that there was no rooms available. Then, she was forced to have her child in a cave used by animals. Oh! How very different that is from us. We need to learn from Mary how to accept the various trials that come to us in life. Mary undoubtedly was more concerned about

Joseph's feelings. After all he was the man of the family and he had seemingly let Mary down. Joseph also took these trials very humbly and without complaint. He surely felt that he should have done better, but how. Both Mary and Joseph had one quality that is lacking in most of us. That is a complete and full trust in God. They did not question why God did not arrange matters in a better manner. They did not blame God for their circumstances. Rather they accepted everything as being God's will. According to the law of Moses, every male child has to be circumcised after eight days of birth. So priests circumcised the child. This ceremony may well have caused some anxiety on the part of Mary. Then the child was officially named Jesus. The name the angel had given Him. Why was it necessary for Jesus to be circumcised? In Genesis, God promised to send someone who would overcome the devil. Because of his perfect obedience, Abraham was made the father of the tribe that would produce this person. Abraham's descendants would be the chosen people of God. The many trials of this people and their failure to remain faithful to God was disappointing. Now, they were awaiting the promised one, the Messiah, the anointed one of God. So this Messiah had to be a member of the Jewish race. Three months after the birth of Jesus, there suddenly appeared three wise men from the east bearing gifts for the newborn king of the Jews. These men were really kings and are called wise men undoubtedly because they were the only ones to foresee the coming of Jesus. There was no welcome for Jesus in the land of Israel. It took these three wise men with their retinue to travel hundreds of miles to not only welcome Jesus but to bring him gifts. The hope and promise for a Messiah is not limited to the Jewish nation only, but applies to all peoples. These wise men were greatly puzzled when no one in Israel knew or even acknowledged the birth of a new king of the Jews. When they spoke to King Herod, the King had to ask the Jewish temple scribes where such a king would be born according to the scriptures. So it was that these wise men were led to Bethlehem. King Herod, of course, wanted no rival to his throne even one as young as a baby. If King Herod had taken these wise men seriously, he would have accompanied them to Bethlehem himself. Sometimes it's necessary for us to have the same kind of faith that these wise men had. Their belief was based on writings and a new star. They blindly followed this star and did not go back even when it was obvious that no one in Israel knew or believed in the birth of a new king of Israel. Our faith is based on something greater than a star, namely Jesus Christ. It is this Jesus that we must follow in our journey here on earth never going to the right or left. Where will this lead us to? Eternal life and happiness with God will be our final destination. Many times in life we look forward to some event or promise only to find that it didn't turn out as we had expected and we become disappointed. Let's consider the reaction of these wise men when they encountered the infant they were searching for. Instead of a royal city, they found a small town in the country. Instead of a royal palace, they found a house which was merely a decorated cave. Instead of a king and queen, they found a young maiden and a carpenter. Yet, they entered with joy to offer their gifts to the baby Jesus. They did not let disappointment or prejudice influence them. We would do well to imitate their example in our relationship with others during our journey here on earth. The first gift given to the infant

Jesus was a small bar of gold. This gift is generally felt to represent the kingship of Jesus. Jesus, the Son of God, is indeed the king of the whole human race. Through his humanity he is one of us and by releasing us from the chains of sin and death, he deservedly is given the kingship over us by his Father. Yet, Jesus is not some remote person who rules over us. He has made us his brothers and sisters. If we remain faithful to him, we become a part of the adopted family of God. This is the real present that Jesus wants which is more valuable to him than all the gold in the world. This is real gold. God loves us and all he asks for is our love in return. The second gift given to Jesus was incense. This gift is generally felt to represent the priesthood of Jesus. Jesus is the only priest capable of offering the only gift pleasing to God the Father which can be accepted for the redemption of all mankind. This is the gift of Himself. Incense has generally been used during sacred ceremonies. It represents the prayers of the worshipers to God. These prayers that we offer up can only be pleasing if they represent our entire will in conformity with the will of God. This is the big and important question we need to ask ourselves daily. Am I doing what God wants and not for any other reason? Our conscience can help us decide but only if it's been well formed according to the teachings of the Church of Jesus here on earth. As scripture tells us, Jesus gave his Church all authority on earth. Just as Jesus led a life of obedience while on earth, he expects his followers to do likewise. The third gift offered was myrrh. This gift was felt to represent the anointing of Jesus after death. Myrrh can also represent mortification and vanquished passions. The death of Jesus resulted not only in our redemption, but also the death of all sin. The road and path to overcoming our attraction to sin whether through the actions of the devil, our weak resistance to sins of the flesh, or the lure of worldly power or riches, lies first and foremost in prayer and fasting. We need to realize with the deepest humility that the only road to eternal life and happiness lies in following God. We do this by listening to the teachings of Jesus given to his Church and by acting on those teachings no matter what the cost is. Many people today long to win money in lotteries, gambling, or any other way. However, Mary and Joseph's reaction to the gifts given to them was much different. They laid them aside and then distributed them to the needy. None of us will attain this high level of detachment from riches, but we can do several things. First, we need to give money and riches a low priority in our life. When blessed with riches, we need to share our wealth with others especially the poor and unfortunate ones in this world. The three kings and their retinue stayed only a few days and then returned to their home countries. They returned by a different route and didn't report to King Herod. We can imagine the spies and soldiers that the King sent to Bethlethem to search out this newborn king. But they could find no one. Certainly the baby born of a poor country woman in a cave couldn't be the one. Joseph and Mary returned to Nazareth and Joseph intended to eventually settle down in the area of Bethlehem after Mary's purification in the Jerusalem temple. This meditation on the birth of Jesus should teach us several different messages. There can be no doubt in our mind of the deep and abiding love that God has for the Blessed Virgin Mary. Yet to bring the Son of God to birth, Mary had to endure a long and certainly unpleasant journey. She and Joseph had to settle for a cave to live in and give birth to Jesus. Yet, there was no complaining or worry during their journey or at the cave. Instead they humbly accepted their hardships without complaint. We can do likewise whenever we find ourselves in situations where events don't go as we would like them to. We too easily get caught up in riches and the cares of the world. Mary and Joseph give us an example of what to strive for in our daily life. God must be the most important person in our life and then we can easily accept whatever may happen to us each day. Mary and Joseph show us that the best use of money or riches is to use it to help the poor and needy. The Old Testament law called for a tithe that is 10 percent to be given to the temple. God promised blessings and happiness to those that did. We would do well to emulate their example. Giving 5 percent to the Church and 5 percent to charities would be a good start. The parents of Mary gave 1/3 to the Temple and 1/3 to the poor and kept 1/3 for themselves. The early Christian church in Jerusalem held all their property and money in common and let the apostles decide on its distribution.

PRESENTATION

A *nd after the days of her purification, according to the law of Moses, were accomplished, they carried him to Jerusalem, to present him to the Lord: As it is written in the law of the Lord: Every male opening the womb shall be called holy to the Lord: And to offer a sacrifice, according as it is written in the law of the Lord, a pair of turtledoves or two young pigeons: And behold there was a man in Jerusalem named Simeon: and this man was just and devout, waiting for the consolation of Israel. And the Holy Ghost was in him. And he had received an answer from the Holy Ghost, that he should not see death before he had seen the Christ of the Lord. And he came by the Spirit into the temple. And when his parents brought in the child Jesus, to do for him according to the custom of the law, He also took him into his arms and blessed God and said: Now thou dost dismiss thy servant, O Lord, according to thy word in peace: Because my eyes have seen thy salvation. Which thou hast prepared before the face of all peoples: A light to the revelation of the Gentiles and the glory of thy people Israel. And his father and mother were wonder-*

ing at those things which were spoken concerning him. And Simeon blessed them and said to Mary his mother: Behold this child is set for the fall and for the resurrection of many in Israel and for a sign which shall be contradicted. And thy own soul a sword shall pierce, that, out of many hearts thoughts may be revealed. And there was one Anna, a prophetess, the daughter of Phanuel, of the tribe of Aser. She was far advanced in years and had lived with her husband seven years from her virginity. And she was a widow until fourscore and four years: who departed not from the temple, by fastings and prayers serving night and day. Now she, at the same hour, coming in, confessed to the Lord: and spoke of him to all that looked for the redemption of Israel. And after they had performed all things according to the law of the Lord, they returned into Galilee, to their city Nazareth. (LK 2: 22-39)

Before the Jews could be released from their slavery by the Egyptians, it was necessary for God to kill the firstborn Egyptian male child and animal before Pharaoh would release them. The Jewish first born male was spared death by the sacrifice of a male lamb during the Passover. The Jewish people celebrated the Passover each year as a result and the first born male was presented to God with a sacrificial animal or bird. So, Jesus was offered up the same as any other firstborn male to God. However, in this case, there is a deeper meaning to this ceremony. Jesus is being offered up also as the future sacrifice for the redemption of the entire human family. Thirty three years later, Jesus will freely offer up himself as this sacrifice which is being performed symbolically now. At this time the Jerusalem Temple would have been crowded with people coming and going. Religious ceremonies were being performed everywhere and into this crowd enters the 15 year old Mary with her baby Jesus and husband Joseph. Mary would be filled with joy as the future Messiah was now to be offered up to God as the Jewish law provided. She undoubtedly had in mind the redemption of her people from Roman occupation. Mary was unaware of the role her son would play in the future redemption of her people and the whole world. Mary enters the Temple full of joy. The priest Simeon took the baby Jesus and performed the necessary offering. What a happy moment for this man who had been told beforehand by the Holy Spirit of the coming of the newly born Messiah. His first words were a blessing to God for allowing him to see this baby and thanksgiving for his coming. He continued with powerful words that proclaimed Jesus the glory of Israel. He also said that he would be a revelation to the gentiles. These are powerful words and certainly nobody at this time could have had any idea what these words meant. These words would imply that a powerful king with a large army would conquer the world like an Alexander the Great. But God does not work like man and the problem is not mastery of people but it is the sins of people that keeps mankind away from God. Simeon gave a hint although he was unaware of its full implication when he spoke of God's Salvation. Everyone at this time was unaware that this Jesus, this tiny baby, was the actual Son of God, God, Himself. Mary and Joseph had no idea what these words of Simeon meant. Mary could have thought that it is a wonderful thing that God will do, and wonder how all of these wonderful events will take place. Simeon blessed Mary because his next words would not be pleasant.

Her son would be the cause of the fall of many. In other words, many would not accept Jesus and they would not be redeemed. We know their rejection of Jesus would mean everlasting death. Simeon also said her son would be the resurrection of many. In other words those who accepted Jesus would rise to everlasting life. The reason is as Simeon puts it a sign that will be contradicted. This sign that Jesus will bring is the sign of the cross. This is the sign that means so much to us. It is our entrance to life with God wherever he is, for where God is there is Heaven. Our ticket to this life is our accepting the sufferings that life gives us just as Jesus did and our accepting Jesus into our lives. These words must have hit Mary like a thunderbolt. Mary, loving and kind, probably never realized the full extent of those who would not accept her son as the Messiah. Since Mary was immaculate, without original sin, her soul feels more deeply than any of us any injuries even those composed of words. Only a rare few people ever experience this partially and then just once or twice. These words of Simeon hit Mary in the deepest recess of her soul. Mary experienced the first of her seven sorrows. As if to confirm what Mary must have now suffered, Simeon told her a sword would pierce her heart. His next words sound somewhat puzzling: "Out of many hearts thoughts may be revealed'. Mary because she was so closely and intimately connected with the life of Jesus, she has been the inspiration of Catholics thoughout the centuries. Though we can never fully imitate her, we look to her life for ways that we can in some small measure follow Jesus. The terrible sorrows that she endured touch many hearts so that they enable many to raise their prayers to Jesus and to follow him just as Mary did. Then another woman, Anna, spoke to all who would listen about this child being the redemption of Israel. What had now taken place in the temple was certainly spoken of throughout the city of Jerusalem and maybe even in some of the outlying countryside. King Herod who had spies everwhere must have certainly heard of the events that had taken place and the talk that was circulating in the city. Meanwhile Mary and Joseph returned to Nazareth. Joseph had intended to resettle in Bethlehem and had made plans to do so. In our meditation we need always to keep in mind that the Mary we are talking about is around 15 years old, young and innocent. Mary because of her immaculate conception was conceived sinless and remained so. This means that Mary enjoyed all the advantages that Adam and Eve had before they sinned. It also means that Mary's body and soul have a closer union with each other. She feels things more deeply than we are capable of doing. A great disadvantage that Mary has is that she is in contact with a very sinful world with many temptations. Today's world is full of rebellion in all phases of life. Rebellion against all sorts of authority. Rebellion in the arts and sciences. Rebellion in religion. St. Paul spoke of this many years ago. So, when we look to Mary what we see is a woman who is the model of obedience. We behold Mary doing whatever God wants her to do and without question. Mary never questions Joseph's actions and does what he tells her. This is undoubtedly the relationship that God had in mind when he created Adam and Eve. Mary was to be the new Eve. Adam and Eve fulfilled their job of increasing mankind in the natural sense. Jesus and Mary were the new Adam and Eve in the sense of bringing mankind to union with God, Jesus by his passion and death and Mary through her obedience and sinless life. When Mary was told all that was to happen to her child Jesus and also to her, her reaction was one of accepting the Will of God. She did not storm heaven and pray that this would not happen. She did not question why or how or when. This is what God has in mind and that was good enough for her. We close this meditation with the next few events. King Herod is enraged when he hears what happened in the temple and he remembers that the three wise men never came back to report to him. He was determined to put an end to this talk of a new king of Israel. Joseph is warned in a dream so he and Mary set out for Egypt in haste. Mary suffers now another deep sorrow at the thought that her child's life was in danger. Simeon's prophesy was being fulfilled in part. King Herod had children two years and younger killed in the region of Bethlehem. Already there were martyrs because of Jesus. Later when Mary heard of this, she must have shed many tears for these poor innocent babies and children. Mary and Joseph stayed in Egypt until King Herod died. Then they returned to Israel. Joseph abandoned the idea of settling in Bethlehem and returned to Nazareth. So the holy family lived the life of immigrants until it was safe to return to their homeland. Mary was ever a model of willing resignation to the will of God.

FINDING

*A*nd the child grew and waxed strong, full of wisdom: and the grace of God was in him. And his parents went every year to Jerusalem, at the solemn day of the pasch. And when he was twelve years old, they going up into Jerusalem, according to the custom of the feast, And having fulfilled the days, when they returned, the child Jesus remained in Jerusalem. And his parents knew it not. And thinking that he was in the company, they came a day's journey and sought him among their kinsfolks and acquaintance. And not finding him, they returned into Jerusalem, seeking him. And came to pass that, after three days, they found him in the temple, sitting in the midst of the doctors, hearing them and asking them questions. And all that heard him were astonished at his wisdom and his answers. And seeing him, they wondered. And his mother said to him: Son, why hast thou done so to us? Behold thy father and I have sought thee sorrowing. And he said to them: How is it that you sought me? Did not know that I must be about my father's business? And they understood not the word that he spoke unto them. And he went down with them and came to Nazareth *and was subject to them. And his mother kept all these words in her heart. And Jesus advanced in wisdom and age and grace with God and men. (LK 2:40-52)*

After the holy family returns from Egypt, we learn that Jesus was growing in age and wisdom and the grace of God was with him. We know that Jesus was both God and man. He had both a human nature complete with a soul and a human will. He also had a divine nature which was one with the Father and the Holy Spirit. What is the interaction of these two natures as Jesus was conceived and growing up? We don't really know. My guess is that the human nature of Jesus progressed normally until the age of reason maybe at 5 or earlier in the case of Jesus. There would be exceptions perhaps when the wise men came or at other times when the Divine nature took over. Nevertheless, Jesus would grow like any normal youth. Since Jesus's human nature would be identical to Adam and Eve's before the fall, he would be endowed with sanctifying grace. One result of this is that his body and soul would be intimately connected so that like Mary he would feel the actions of others very deeply not only physically and mentally, but also in the very depths of his being. The event we are meditating on is a very strange one indeed. It results in the third sorrow of Mary and the fifth joyfull mystery. As youths enter their teenage years, they begin to want to strongly imitate adults. They want to be grownup. They want to imitate their father. Jesus would seem to be no different in this respect. The big question is why did Jesus elude his parents instead of just asking their permission? Remember that both Joseph and Mary were not aware that Jesus was God, Himself. They probably would have told him to come with them and not given their permission. And Jesus could not disobey his parents. The Bible does not say much about what Jesus really did for three days in the Temple. So let us listen to the visions recorded by Anna Catharina Emmerick about this event. She states that Jesus joined several youths and went with them to three schools, two in the city and the last in the Temple. These schools taught other branches besides that of the Law. Jesus questioned the doctors and rabbis of these schools and his answers astonished and embarrassed them This was so true that they resolved to humble this boy Jesus. They gathered the rabbis most deeply versed in the various sciences from these schools and met with Jesus in the public lecture hall of the temple on the afternoon of the third day. Jesus had previously illustrated his answers and explanations by all kinds of examples from nature, art, and science. The scribes and doctors had gathered together masters in all these branches and now one by one they began to dispute with him. Jesus remarked that while such subjects did not appear appropriate to the Temple, he would discuss them since it was his Father's will. Now they imagined that he was refering to Joseph and not his heavenly Father. They figured Joseph had wanted Jesus to show off his learning. Jesus answered and taught upon medicine and he described the whole human body in a way far beyond the understanding of the most learned one. He did the same with astronomy, architecture, agriculture, geometry, arithmetic, jurisprudence, and every other subject put to him. He applied his knowledge skillfully to the Law and the Promise, to the Prophecies, to the Temple, to the mysteries of worship and sacrifice so that his hearers were confounded. They went from astonishment and admiration to fury and shame. Meanwhile, Mary and Joseph finally entered the Temple and inquired about their Child and were told that he was in the lecture hall. Since they could not enter the lecture hall, they sent a levite to call Jesus. Jesus sent word that he must first finish what he was about. Mary was very much troubled since he didn't obey at once for this was the first time he gave his parents to understand that he had other commands rather than theirs to fulfill. While Joseph kept a humble silence, Mary questioned Jesus as to why he did this as they looked for him sorrowfully. Jesus answered gravely why did you search for me. He said: "Did you not know that I must be about my Father's business." But they did not understand him. We can imagine that when Mary went looking for Jesus, she would be like any other mother who has suddenly lost her child and is then desperately searching for her child. The sorrow that Mary felt must have been very deep and hit her very hard. Yet in spite of her sorrow, Mary looked for Jesus with hope and resignation to the will of God. She had always placed her hope in the Almighty and she knew he would not abandon her now. Mary's example should be a model for us to look at. We should understand that God is always there with us and no matter the outcome we can be sure that the right outcome will take place. We must not overlook the role of Joseph in this matter. He, no less than Mary, would search sorrowfully for Jesus. The responsibility for his son falls on the head of the family. Like Mary, Joseph also put his trust in God for he would know full well that this child of Mary is destined for some great task by God. It would be hard for us to imagine the total happiness and joy that Mary experienced when she and Joseph finally found Jesus. We cannot let the events overshadow this happening. Each of us can remember some event that happened in our lives that brought us some great happiness. Yet let us put this event in its proper perspective. The true and total happiness that we should all be looking forward to is our being united with Jesus in our next life after death. It is only then that we shall experience true happiness for all eternity. If we are not careful, we can easily lose the path to true happiness when we lose our way through sin.. This life is full of many traps and enticements. The world is calling us to enjoy life with its sinful pleasures. It's so easy to want to get ahead in the world. Why not a bigger car or a bigger house? Why not make millions of dollars? It can be done but at what cost. Remember what Jesus said. What does it profit a man to gain the whole world and suffer the loss of his soul? We must maintain a true perspective on life and that can only be done if we keep our eyes on Jesus. We know that the true path to Jesus is marked out for us by his Holy Catholic Church. Sometimes in spite of our best intentions, we lose our way. We have lost Jesus and we desperately search to find him. In this world of ours there are literally thousands of religions calling out that their religion is the one to follow. Many religions teach that it doesn't matter what religion you follow as they are all the same. It would be impossible to list all of them and check their various credentials. However, we can simplify the task considerably. A God who is so smart and capable of creating the world and a human race would surely leave a record of his creation dating back to the beginning. The only religions to have such a credible record is Judaism and Christianity. The difference between the two is that Judaism rejects Jesus as their Messiah while Christianity accepts him. The covenant between God and Judaism would seem to be over as there is no Temple, no daily sacrifice of any kind, and no High Priest. The Catholic Church is the only branch of Christianity which can trace itself back to the followers of Jesus, St. Peter and the Apostles. Furthermore its doctrines have developed but have not changed from the times of the Apostles. In spite of troubles both within and without the Church it has survived to the present day. There is a continuous record of miracles being performed by various members of the Catholic Church during each of the previous centuries to the present day. Furthermore, Mary has appeared to some members of the Church in various apparitions over the last few centuries. So when we are lost and are looking for Jesus, we will find him in the teaching of the Catholic Church which perfectly conforms to the teachings of Jesus that will be found in the Bible. It should be noted that taking individual sentences and phrases of the words of Jesus instead of the total message of Jesus can result in a different understanding of the teaching of Jesus. When Jesus went obediently with Mary and Joseph back to their home in Nazareth, Mary kept all these things in her heart. She did not understand what Jesus meant about obeying his Father. She knew it wasn't Joseph. It probably never dawned on her that it was God. Jesus went back and was the obedient son of the carpenter, Joseph, and his mother, Mary. These must have been happy days for this holy family as they passed their days in work and prayer. God does not hurry our salvation, but shows us the patience that is sometimes necessary for a good work to come about. While we do not know anything about this part of the life of Jesus, we can imagine that he was preparing himself for the great task that only he was aware of. This is a model of how we should go about our life accepting what comes to us and remaining a close member of our family, a family joyfully united in prayer. Jesus reaches the age of 30 and the time for him to act has come. The joyful times for Mary are over. Soon it will be time for Jesus to enlighten the world about his true nature.

BAPTISM

*A*nd it came to pass, in those days, Jesus came from Nazareth of Galilee and was baptized by John in the Jordan. And forthwith coming up out of the water, he saw the heavens opened and the Spirit as a dove descending and remaining on him. And there came a voice from heaven: Thou art my beloved Son; in thee I am well pleased. And immediately the Spirit drove him out into the desert. (MK 1:9-12)

John the Baptist seems a strange figure indeed. Driven from his home when Herod tried to kill the baby Jesus, John went into the desert where he lived until he was 30 years old. Only with the help of God could he have survived living only on what he could find in the desert. All this time we can imagine that he was instructed by the Holy Spirit and perhaps aided by angels. This life of strict penance was necessary to demonstrate to the people the terrible consequences of sin. John's life and preaching demonstrated to the people that he was indeed a prophet. To prepare the Jewish people for the coming of the Messiah, Jesus, it was necessary for the people to acknowledge their sins and to ask for forgiveness. John the Baptist came and asked the people to repent of their sins and to show their repentance by being baptized in the Jordan River by John. This baptism by John did not take away any sin, but was a sign that the person being baptized was sorry for his sins and that he resolved not to sin anymore. Thus John was able to cause the people to pause and think about the life they were leading and to lead them to repentance for their sins. It takes a courageous person to speak out against the sins of the leaders as many people were afraid to speak out. How true this is in our own age when so many leaders including clergy find it so easy to take the easy road of excuses for not speaking out. We must resolve to remain faithful no matter what it costs us. Jesus's kind and merciful words were always followed by sharp words against those who were hypocritical in practicing their faith. We cannot truly call ourselves a follower of Christ if we are not ready to boldly proclaim the truth. Let us pray for the courage and strength to persevere in our love of Jesus. When Jesus approached John he was only one of many persons who had come to be baptized. He looked to be an ordinary Jew. Now Jesus did not have any need to repent of his sins because he was sinless. Why did he do this? Because he not only wanted to give us an example, but also because he represented the whole human race. Those of us who are sorry for the sins we have committed are represented by Jesus. You and I are there with Jesus. John immediately recognized Jesus as the Messiah and protested that Jesus should rather baptize him. John knew he was unworthy to baptize Jesus. However Jesus told him it was necessary to do so. So, John immediately baptized Jesus. The baptism of Jesus becomes more than a sign for us. It is the anointing of Jesus by the Holy Spirit for the mission of redemption which Jesus came on earth to accomplish. This event marked the first time that the Trinity was revealed. The Father said that this was his beloved Son and the Holy Spirit appeared in the form of a dove. The water of the world was cleansed by Jesus so that in the future it could be used as the outward sign of Christian Baptism. Having been anointed by the Holy Spirit, Jesus was now ready to begin his mission. He had been anointed by his heavenly Father. Now what must Jesus do to begin his journey to the cross? Jesus then went into the desert where he fasted and prayed. The Son of God unlike us was not to rush out and start his mission. He went out to the desert to fast and pray. The Bible points out that fasting cures a multitude of sins. The great weapons against temptation and sin are prayer, fasting, and almsgiving. The human nature of Jesus would be sorely tempted during the three years of his mission and he needed all the help he could muster. We are currently living in the greatest age of evil and temptation. To survive, we must live a heroic life of virtue. There is only one way to survive and that is to follow the example of Jesus. Daily prayer at morning, evening, and at night is a must. Fasting when possible will help. Attending Sunday Mass and other Masses, if possible, is also a must. Movies, television, and the media all sound the seductive call of sin and evil. Wrong actions are justified as rights. History is changed to conform to current forms of correctness. We cannot be Catholic and do nothing. We need to follow the example of Jesus. After forty days of fasting and prayer, Jesus, being human, becomes hungry. It is then that the devil appears. Jesus is weak and now is the time when the devil chooses to act against this Messiah. He does not know that Jesus is the Son of God in human form. Jesus is attacked the same way that we are, although many times we are not aware that the devil is behind the temptation. We must always be on guard and use prayer to protect us from evil. There are three major temptations that a person can be subjected to: the world, the devil, and the flesh. Everyone of us can relate to having experienced one or more of these temptations many times and probably none of us could ever think that the devil tempted him. The first temptation that the devil used was that of the flesh. Jesus was tempted to use his power as a Messiah to satisfy his hunger. The devil told Jesus to change the stones into bread. Then Jesus could gorge himself on the bread. Hungry though he was, Jesus told the devil that man does not live on bread alone, but by every word of God. Jesus turns his temptation into a sermon. Yes, man needs bread and food to survive, but to survive is not enough. We need to live by the word of God. This word of God is not just the Bible, it is Jesus, Himself. Jesus by his life and actions teaches us the true life we need to live. The second temptation of the devil was that of the world. Jesus was led to a high mountain not only so that he could see the kingdoms, but also he could experience the power of being the ruler. In a moment of time, he was shown all the kingdoms of the world and told he could have them with all their power and glory if Jesus would adore him. Notice that the devil said he could give them to Jesus. Was he lying or does the glory and powers of the kingdoms of this world belong to the devil? Certainly, when we consider the many wars and killings that many governments do, we could believe that at least the spirit of the devil was behind them. Jesus answered the devil by telling him that only God is to be adored and served. The choice could not be clearer. Do we serve and adore God or the world? Many popular people have fans who seem to adore them instead of God. The world has many temptations: fame, money, power, and entertainment. These temptations can easily be sought while ignoring God completely. Everyone wants to be successful but there is a temptation to go to excess. So long as we place God first then whatever success we enjoy is sufficient. The greater we rise in the eyes of the world, the greater the danger. Our eyes must always be on Christ. The third temptation was by the devil himself. He took Jesus to the highest point of the temple in Jerusalem and told him to throw himself down. After all, the devil explained, scripture says that the angels will protect him from harm. Jesus points out that scripture also says that you should not tempt the Lord, your God. Now, the devil had reference to Jesus as the Messiah and not as God, for no one at this time knew that Jesus was the Son of God, including the devil. This temptation by the devil is hard for us to understand mainly because the devil likes to keep himself hidden. His temptations are likewise hidden and we are probably never aware of their cause. Notice in this temptation that the devil leads Jesus to the Jerusalem temple where the glory of God resides in a special way. He quotes scripture to Jesus. It is so easy to be led astray in religious matters unless we are taught by a legitimate teaching authority. Jesus gave his authority to Peter and the Apostles verbally. This authority was passed on orally to the leaders of his Church, the Catholic Church. Some of the Apostles and disciples of Jesus wrote down some of the events in the life of Jesus as well as some of the sermons of Jesus. In the fourth century, the Church determined which writing by the Apostles and disciples of Jesus were authentic and collected them in the New Testament. The New Testament together with the Old Testament makes up the Bible which is the reference book of the Catholic Church. It should be clear that Christians who wish to follow Jesus would look to the Catholic Church for their guidance in morals and religious matters. It is not easy many times to live the life that Jesus wants us to live. It calls for prayer and sacrifice. Many religions talk about the good things in being a Christian, but Jesus always emphasized the sacrifices. One must go through the passion before the resurrection.

MIRACLE

*A*nd the third day, there was a marriage in Cana of Galilee: and the mother of Jesus was there. And Jesus also was invited, and his disciples, to the marriage. And the wine failing, the mother of Jesus saith to him: They have no wine. And Jesus saith to her: Woman, what is that to me and to thee? My hour is not yet come. His mother saith to the waiters: Whatsoever he shall say to you, do ye. Now there were set there six waterpots of stone, according to the manner of the purifying of the Jews, containing two or three measures apiece. Jesus saith to them: Fill the waterpots with water. And they filled them up to the brim. And Jesus saith to them: Draw out now and carry to the chief steward of the feast. And they carried it. And when the chief steward had tasted the water made wine and knew not whence it was, but the waiters knew who had drawn the water: the chief steward calleth the bridegroom, And saith to him: Every man at first setteth forth good wine, and when men have well drunk, then that which is worse. But thou hast kept the good wine until now. This beginning of miracles did

Jesus in Cana of Galilee and manifested his glory. And his disciples believed in him. (JN 2: 1-11)

Our meditation will draw on the visions of Anna Catharina Emmerick. The wedding feast of one of the relatives of Jesus was in Cana of Galilee. The family of the couple were very well to do and the wedding party had over one hundred guests, mostly relatives, and included friends of Jesus as well as his disciples. Would Jesus at a wedding feast with his relatives and disciples stay in the background as a bystander? Is this logical? Of course not. Jesus was to use this occasion as a means for his followers to get acquainted with his relatives as well as his usual means of teaching spiritual lessons. As one can imagine, Jesus was active in mixing with the people, helping with the games, and interspersing them with spiritual lessons. He would give private advice to many persons especially the bride and groom. This wedding feast lasted many days. Jesus supplied the second course of the meal at the banquet as well as the wine. When Mary saw that the wine had failed, she reminded Jesus that he had said that he would provide the wine. Jesus's answer to Mary seems strange to us. We must remember that we were not there and we probably have only part of the conversation. Jesus addressed Mary as woman not as mother because he was to perform an action full of mystery as the Messiah and the Son of God. Here we see Mary performing her role as mediatrix for the first time. A role that she would play in the act of salvation by Jesus. A role that she continues even to this present day. The wine that Jesus was about to provide was more than ordinary wine, it was a symbol of that mystery when he would change wine into his own Blood. The statement of

Jesus that his hour had not come, contains three meanings. First, the hour for Jesus to supply the promised wine. Second, the hour for Jesus to change the water into wine. Third, the hour for changing wine into his own Blood. Notice what happens next. Mary tells the servants to do whatever Jesus tells them to do. Mary does the same thing today. When we pray to her for help, she talks to her Son and our petition is answered. Sometimes we imagine that it was not, but it may only be delayed to a better time. Sometimes we are given a better solution. Sometimes the answer is no as God knows best what is good for us. But in all cases we can be sure that God has the perfect solution for us. We need to act like Mary did with perfect confidence in what Jesus will do. Remember that Mary had no idea how Jesus would solve the problem Three water jugs and three wine jugs were brought to Jesus and inverted over a basin to be sure that they were empty. Notice that the jugs were filled to the brim with water. When God does something he does not do it halfway, but completes it to the brim. After Jesus blesses the water, he tells the servant to bring a cup of the changed water to the steward. The steward was surprised that the wine was so good and he told the bridegroom that the good wine is served first and the poorer wine later, but that he had saved the best wine for last. Now no one except the family of the bridal pair knew that Jesus was to provide the wine for the wedding. Then, great was the surprise of the bridegroom and the bride's father when they drank the wine. The servants protested that they had only drawn water and the drinking vessels and glasses on the table had been filled with the same. Now the whole company drank. The result of this is not excitement, but a spirit of silent awe and reverence. Jesus uses this occasion to teach those present about this miracle. The world presents the strong wine first and then deceives the partially intoxicated with bad drinks. It was not to be that way in the Kingdom that his Heavenly Father had given him. There, pure water was changed to costly wine so that lukewarmness should give place to ardor and intrepid zeal. Jesus taught them about the future Eucharist using parables so that they would not fully understand what he was saying. Thus for the first time Jesus spoke of his future mission and demonstrated his power and dignity. This company of relatives and disciples could be looked upon as the first community of Jesus's followers, the first Christians. Jesus's presence and actions at this wedding feast had a profound effect on all those present and undoubtedly carried over into their future lives especially for the future Apostles who were present. Yet all this occurred because of the miracle of water changed into wine. While the wine was undoubtedly exceptional, it was still nonetheless ordinary wine. Today we can be present at an ordinary Mass when an even greater miracle takes place. The priest, endowed with the power given to him by the Church of God, changes ordinary wine into the Blood of Jesus. And we can drink this precious blood which provides spiritual life to us if we are receptive to it. There is no greater miracle on earth than this. We can drink this with joy because while it retains all the characteristics of wine, the substance has changed into the Blood of Jesus. This is the Blood that was shed for the remission of our sins. This Blood was shed not only to wipe away the Original sin of Adam, but also all our personal sins as well. Let us consider for a moment, how we prepare to receive this great sacrament given to us by our Lord. Certainly, we would not want to visit a special friend's house with dirty clothes and filthy shoes. Would we then ask Jesus to enter our dirty body filled with unrepentent sins. No, we must be sure that we are worthy to receive our Lord. The first step is to be truly sorry for all the sins we have committed in the past especially the ones with which we have become attached to. It is not enough to want to avoid hell, we must be sorry for our sins because they offend Jesus. Is Jesus really offended by my sins? Look at the crucifix. Would Jesus really go through that much pain and suffering if it didn't matter if I sinned or not? Jesus offers us eternal life and happiness and to obtain that for us he underwent a terrible amount of suffering and pain. Do we really care? Jesus has provided in his Church a means for us to confess our sins in privacy so that no one will know them except God who then promptly forgets them. Before receiving the sacrament of Penance, one should examine their conscience to be sure that they are prepared to confess all their sins even the ones that they are most ashamed of. A person should be sure that there is complete understanding of what the Church teaches about what is and is not a sin. No one can go against the teachings of the Church because Jesus has guaranteed that the Church is teaching his truths. While confessing our sins wipes the slate clean, we need to ensure that we will not remain empty. We need to bring Jesus into our lives and there is no better way to do that than by prayer. Not only do we need to pray daily, but we need to pray several times each day. While we work or play or amuse ourselves, we need to be sure that we fill our minds and hearts with thoughts of God. An empty mind and heart is an invitation for the devil and evil thoughts. The highlight of every week should be the Sunday Mass. Just think, Jesus, himself, waits for you to come so that at communion time, he can get closer to you than any other human being by actually entering your body when you eat his Body and drink his Blood at Holy Communion. At that moment you are one with your God. He is spirit and you are his creature. During Mass, your thoughts and actions should be directed toward that great moment when you will go forward to receive Jesus in the Blessed Sacrament of Holy Eucharist. Afterwards, you can communicate with God as few people can because you know that He is there within you. This mystery is the beginning of Jesus's teaching mission to the world. It was a wonderful start with his relatives, friends, and disciples. If we have not already begun to know and love God, today is a good time to begin. And if we have begun, we surely can do more. God loves us so much and he has demonstrated his love through his passion and death on the cross. Through this action, he has also demonstrated the terrible effects of sin. There was no other way for God to reconcile mankind with Himself. The way to a heavenly life with God is open to all persons. Now, it's up to each person to choose which path to take.

MESSAGE

*A*nd *after that John was delivered up, Jesus came
into Galilee, preaching the gospel of the kingdom of God. And saying: The time is accomplished and
the kingdom of God is at hand. Repent and believe the
gospel. (MK 1:14-15)*

Jesus was now confronted with the large task of con-
vincing the Jewish people that he was indeed the Messiah that they were looking for. His task was compounded
by the fact that what the people were awaiting is an
earthly Messiah. A Messiah that would crush the Roman
conquerors and rule the world thus bringing in a time of
peace and prosperity. And who could blame them as the
messages given them by the prophets can well be interpreted that way. Completely ignored by the people was
the primary cause of man's troubles in the world, the sin
of Adam and Eve. Jesus had gathered a small band of
twelve Apostles and followers who had accepted his
teachings with faith. It was now time for Jesus to take his
message to the Jewish people because they were chosen
to spread this message to the world. John the Baptist had

prepared the way through his preaching of penance and his announcement of the coming of the Messiah. It is well for us to learn from this that what is important is not what we may have followed through tradition in our families or organizations, but what it is that God wants us to do. Unless the religion or faith that we practice is in conformity with what God wants, then we are not doing what God wants but what we want. A religion can become so comfortable that we can fool ourselves into believing that we are following the will of God. A person that truly loves God will not rest until he knows that he is following the path that God has marked out for him. Jesus's teachings were passed on to the Apostles orally who in turn passed them down to us today through their successors, the Bishops. The gospel writers wrote a summary of the teachings and not in any particular order. It was important that the principal teachings of Jesus be passed on to the people through the Church that Jesus founded. This would include a summary of the events of Jesus's life. These writings known as the New Testament were added to the Old Testament books. These scripture books known as the Bible were to be in effect the reference book of the Church which can only be properly interpreted by the successors of the apostles. Jesus begins his preaching mission by proclaiming that the time has come to repent and believe the good news. The good news or gospel is that the kingdom of God is within you. The Jews were looking for an external kingdom, an earthly kingdom. Jesus was preaching an internal and spiritual kingdom that is inside every person. This kingdom can be attained only by obeying the word of God. Jesus is the word of God. This connection will not be made by the followers of Jesus until after the death and resurrection of Jesus. The people wondered about Jesus because he spoke with authority. The scribes and Pharisees taught by quoting various rabbis teachings about certain passages of the Bible and their meanings. Jesus being the Son of God knew exactly what the meaning of scripture passages was. An important lesson for us here is that every word that Jesus utters has a meaning and can't be ignored because we don't like it. The teachings of Jesus about eating his Body and Blood turned many people away including some of his disciples. Did Jesus correct them and say that he was speaking figuratively? No. Instead, he turned to the Apostles and asked them if they were going also. It was only later at the Last Supper that the true meaning of his words were revealed. Jesus had one powerful tool to bring his message to the Jewish people and that was his natural ability to work miracles. However, Jesus showed his sympathy for others by his working miracles to cure people of their sickness, heal their deformities, and expel demons. Several times he brought people back to life from the dead. All this was but a means for Jesus to draw everyone to his true purpose and that was the forgiveness of sins through faith in Himself. We see several times that Jesus says your faith has saved you. In one particular incident, Jesus does not cure the person immediately but instead says that his sins are forgiven. Several Jewish leaders question this declaration saying that only God can forgive sins. They are correct as Jesus is God. He demonstrates this by curing the man as only God can work a miracle by his own power. Unfortunately, the Jewish leaders don't make the connection. Sometimes we have the same problem as we don't wish to connect the teaching of Jesus with the living of our lives. A tradition had evolved among the

Jewish leaders of applying the laws of Moses down to the tiniest degree and making it mandatory for all the people. Jesus pointed out that the laws were made for man, not man for the laws. We can be guilty of the same thing in our observance of our religious practices. Our religious practices need to be tailored to our regular life whether we are a religious, a worker, or a housewife. Our prayer life must not interfere with our necessary relationship with others especially those in need. God wished his people to be free from sin that is impure. This idea is shown by their rituals of cleansing themselves before eating as an example. Jesus pointed out to them that what was more important was the internal cleansing of each individual. It is what comes from the heart and mind of each person that determines whether that person is pure or not. In the world of today where there is so much sexual impurity, we need to be careful that we do not imitate the world but rather Jesus. There is a tendency today to minimize the effects of sin. Jesus did not do this. He was very clear about the ultimate punishment due to an unrepentant sinner. In almost every recorded sermon, he had harsh words for those who refused to turn away from their sins. It is really a matter of justice to show everyone the consequences of their way of life. The way of an unrepentant sinner is eternal fire and suffering. The way of the followers of Jesus is eternal happiness in the next life. The timid need not be afraid that they are not doing enough as Jesus knows full well our limitations and he will take that into account with his great mercy. The greatest of the virtues is humility which God demonstrated by becoming a man even though he was divine. Jesus, the second Person of the Trinity, demonstrated this virtue during the three years of his preaching. Rather than making a big show of his miracle working ability, Jesus downplayed it in many subtle ways. He would draw the person out from the crowd. He would perform a miracle with only a few persons present. He would tell the cured person not to tell anyone. How different this is from us as we want to shout out our great accomplishments to the whole world. The road to holiness begins with humility and we need to go down this road if we really want to follow Jesus. An important part of the life of Jesus is prayer. This is somewhat confusing. If Jesus is God, then he is praying to himself. This does not seem to make sense. While Jesus is God, the second Person of the Trinity, in his divine nature, this nature is pure spirit. Jesus has a human nature which he received from his earthly mother, Mary. This human nature includes body, soul, spirit, and free will. This means that the humanity of Jesus needs to closely talk or pray to God the Father. To us this is a great mystery that is beyond our understanding. At one time Jesus made it clear that even he did not know when the end of the world would take place. So, it would seem that God withheld this information from the humanity of Jesus. The most important message from all this is the necessity of prayer in our lives. Jesus sometimes spent all night in prayer and we find it difficult to spend even 10 minutes. What are the effects of prayer? First of all, it shows our love for God. Does a lover never talk to the loved one? Of course not. The more we talk to a person, the more we get to know that person and the more we get to love that person. Jesus said that if we had faith enough, we could actually move a mountain. So prayer will help us increase our faith. Life is sometimes difficult and we need help. God is there always ready to help us in the trials that we undergo in life. Jesus points out to us that to follow him, we must take up our cross daily just as he did. So the question that we ask ourselves is how does this benefit me. It is human nature to want to know what benefit we will get by following Jesus. Now, a person who truly loves Jesus as he or she should, does not want anything. That is what pure love is like. However, Jesus offers us the greatest gift we could possibly wish for: eternal life. Remember Adam and Eve had eternal life until they sinned. If we follow Jesus faithfully, then he promises us eternal life even greater than Adam and Eve because we will see God face to face. If we are not faithful, then we will go to a region of hell in the next life which is really not like living life itself. This is something that Jesus was very clear about. Our bodies will be united with our souls at the end of the world and the faithful ones will live a happy life in a new world free from all sin and death. If we are to enjoy this new life with God as Jesus promises, then it is very important to our eternal salvation that we know what we must do to obtain this new life. Jesus tells us that he is the way, the truth, and the life. The teachings of Jesus can be interpreted in many different ways especially if taken out of context. It is a matter of life and death to get it correct. Fortunately, Jesus established a Church when he told Peter that he was the rock on which Jesus would build his Church. This Church with Peter as its first leader has existed to the present day and will continue to exist until the end of time. The true meaning of the teachings of Jesus are faithfully preserved in this Church, the Catholic Church. Jesus promised he would be with them always and through the Holy Spirit, the teachings of Jesus have been kept unchanged. While it has been necessary at times to clarify or expand the teachings, they remain unchanged. It is clear that if we love Jesus, then we will love his Church. We will not let anything go between us and his Church. And what is this Church? It is the Pope and Bishops united to the Pope and all of the faithful Catholics united to the Pope. This is what Jesus wants and so we should do everything we can to learn all about our faith. We practice our faith by participating in Mass where we meet Jesus in the Eucharist. The Eucharist is our ticket to eternal life as Jesus promised us. Why? Because we show our great love for Jesus by allowing him to come into our hearts through the Eucharist.

TRANSFIGURATION

A nd after six days, Jesus taketh unto him Peter and James, and John his brother, and bringeth them up into a high mountain apart. And he was transfigured before them. And his face did shine as the sun: and his garments became white as snow. And behold there appeared to them Moses and Elias talking with him. And Peter answering, said to Jesus: Lord, it is good for us to be here: if thou wilt, let us make here three tabernacles, one for thee, and one for Moses, and one for Elias. And as he was yet speaking, behold a bright cloud overshadowed them. And lo, a voice out of the cloud, saying: This is my beloved Son in whom I am well pleased. Hear ye him. And the disciples hearing, fell upon their face and were very much afraid. And Jesus came and touched them and said to them: Arise and fear not. And they lifting up their eyes saw no one but only Jesus. And as they came down from the mountain, Jesus charged them, saying: Tell the vision to no man till the Son of man be risen from the dead. (MT 17: 1-9)

Eight days before the Transfiguration, Jesus tells his disciples that some of them would not taste death till they see the kingdom of God. Two days later Jesus and his disciples celebrated the Passover together and six days after that they arrived at the foot of Mount Tabor. Jesus had everyone wait at the bottom of Mount Tabor except for Peter, James, and John who traveled with him to the top of the mountain where they spent the night. In the morning then, the Transfiguration of Jesus took place. The three Apostles were the ones who would see the kingdom of God before their death because Jesus glorified is the kingdom of God. Jesus had told us that the kingdom of God is within us. This truth is hidden to us and we have to accept it on faith. The three apostles see this kingdom as it will appear when this current world of ours is ended. It's easy to understand why Jesus showed his glory at this time. He was on his final journey to Jerusalem for the Passover in which he would be the victim. Jesus would show them who he was in all his glory so that they would not waver in faith when they would see him during his passion and death. While this event had a great impression on the three Apostles, it was shortlived as future events would demonstrate. However, after the descent of the Holy Spirit, the apostles could relate to this event which would strengthen the hope of all Christians in the final resurrection. While the apostles are somewhat dumfounded while Moses and Elijah appear and speak with Jesus, they nevertheless can hear what they are talking about. Jesus was telling them in detail about his coming passion and death that he would incur in Jerusalem. If there was ever any doubt in the minds of the three Apostles about the identity of Jesus, it was now dispelled. Jesus was surely the Messiah that the scrip-

tures foretold and that the Jews were awaiting. This event
on Mount Tabor should give us hope for our future life
after death if we remain faithful. Just as Jesus was transfigured, we also will be transfigured though not with the
same glory. Our bodies will become perfect without any
defects. We will be immortal and we will be full of sanctifying grace. We will see God face to face and we will
have no inclination to sin. Life for everyone will be
beyond their wildest expectations. If we die with Christ,
then we shall also live with Christ. This is our expectation. This is our hope. There are times when things are
just not going well for us and it is at these times that we
should remember the transfiguration of Jesus. This is
what we are working towards. Our main motivation
should be our love for Jesus. This does not mean that we
cannot look forward toward a future and wonderful life
in the world to come. We should not be like these Apostles who wondered what rising from the dead meant as
they traveled down the mountain. They just didn't get it
yet in spite of all the efforts of Jesus to tell them. Their
minds were simply closed. Are we the same way when it
comes to the teachings of Jesus as given to us by his
Church? We need to ensure that our conscience is in tune
with the teachings of the Church because these teachings
are the teachings of God, Himself. If our conscience con-
flicts with the Church's teachings, then it's obvious that
we need to reexamine our conscience and bring it into
agreement with the teachings of Jesus. It's easy to want
to have things our way and to be stubborn and insist that
the Church is wrong in this or that matter. The truth is
that it is we who are wrong not God's Church. When
Jesus and the three Apostles reached the foot of the
mountain, an episode occurred that deserves our atten-

tion. A small boy possessed by a demon was rolling on the ground. The disciples were unable to drive the demon out. Jesus first words were directed to the father. He accused him of unbelief. The father pleaded "Lord I do believe, help my unbelief!" Jesus then healed the boy by driving the demon out. Isn't this like us at times when we want something and we pray for it and then don't receive it. We think that we have faith, but deep in our heart we really don't believe. Let us pray to God that he will give us the faith that we need to trust him always. Faith doesn't come without many prayers and charitable acts of kindness. The disciples wonder why they could not drive the demon out. It seems that they lacked faith themselves. Jesus goes on to tell them them that this sort of action is only accomplished by prayers and fasting. It could well be that the disciples had forgotten that it is by the action of God that they are able to do the works of God. He needs to be invoked. When doing the acts of God, he needs to be acknowledged. We learn from sacred Scripture that there are three things that pleases God: prayer, fasting, and almsgiving. Everyone of us can practice these tools that God has given us to increase our faith and allow us to lead the good lives that God wishes. After the Transfiguration, Jesus is on the journey to his passion and death in Jerusalem which is his ultimate mission. Jesus frequently talks of his impending death, but the Apostles just don't seem to get the message. Sometimes we don't get the message about the life we need to live in order to please God and reach heaven. We just can't be Sunday Catholics and think that we're doing enough to get us into heaven. In these perilous times we need to live lives of heroic virtue because all around us the values of the world will lead us in the opposite direction. Just think how discouraged that Jesus must have been when his two top apostles, James and John, approach him and ask for a favor. They want to sit at his right and left hand in the kingdom that Jesus will rule. You and I would not exhibit the patience that Jesus did. Jesus asked them if they would drink the chalice that he would drink. They said we can. Jesus tells them that they will. Then Jesus pointed out that it was not his to give. In reading the Gospels, we tend to wonder how the Apostles could be so ignorant. We even fancy that we would certainly get the message. But we did not live in that time and that culture. We live in the present culture and time and there are all sorts of wrong and misleading messages being sent to us. Are we really reading them correctly so as to reject those which are contrary to the teaching of Jesus which we receive from the Church. The Church's teachings come to us from the Pope and the Bishops who are in union with him. Any messages or teachings contrary to those teachings even if they come from members of the Church are false teachings. Jesus has worked many miracles giving evidence of his divinity. Even his critics admitted that his works showed the power of God, but they just did not put the two together. When Jesus forgave the sins of a paralyzed man, the Pharisees said who can forgive sins except God. Jesus then showed his power as God by curing the paralyzed man. The wind and sea obeyed him and he walked on water. He cured the sick and lame. He expelled demons from possessed persons. He raised dead persons to life. He cured in many different ways and even from a distance. It was on this final journey that Jesus worked his greatest miracle. Jesus hears that his good friend Lazarus was ill and he remarks that this sickness will end not in death, but in

God's glory and that through it the Son of God will be glorified. Yet instead of going to the home of Lazarus, Jesus stayed where he was for two more days. At this time Jesus was not in Judaea, but on the other side of the Jordan River. He then said: "Let's go to Judaea." Jesus tells them that Lazarus is dead. Knowing that the Jews wanted to kill Jesus, Thomas says," Lets go too, and die with him." Arriving at the home of Lazarus, they learn that he has been dead for four days. Jesus goes to the tomb and asks for the stone to be rolled out. Martha, the sister of Lazarus, protests saying that by now he would smell badly. Jesus insists and they roll the stone over and Jesus tells Lazarus to come out. He comes out and they remove his burial cloths. This is a stupendous miracle. No one can claim that he really was not dead as he was four days in the tomb and they could see the corruption on the burial cloths. As a result of this miracle, many Jews were converted. The Jewish leaders were at a loss as to what to do. Their high priest, Caiphas, said," You don't seem to have grasped the situation at all; you fail to see that it is better for one man to die for the people, than for the whole nation to be destroyed." The stage was now set for Jesus to be killed. The only question was how and when. Jesus had one more great and public event to accomplish before the start of his passion. The crowds of Jews had heard that Jesus was coming into Jerusalem and they went to meet him. Jesus rode in on a donkey to shouts of Hosanna Blessings on the King of Israel who comes in the name of the Lord. They greeted him with branches of palms. The whole city turned out and there was euphoria in the air. The message for us here is that there are times when it seems like everything is great and glorious and we are so happy. However, we know that things can change very quickly and we always need to be on our guard and realize that nothing in this world really lasts. It is only in the next world which we are awaiting that we can be truly happy. Padre Pio had a saying that is worthwhile for us to adopt: Pray, Hope, and don't worry.

EUCHARIST

A *nd taking bread, he gave thanks and brake and gave to them, saying: This is my body, which is given for you. Do this for a commemoration of me. In like manner, the chalice also, after he had supped, saying: This is the chalice, the new testament in my blood, which shall be shed for you. (LK 22: 19-20)*

Jesus has finished the three years of his public teaching and the time had come for him to say farewell to his closest friends, the Apostles. The Apostles who are appointed by Jesus to be the leaders of his Church, have not completely accepted or understood what Jesus has been trying to teach them in the past three years. Recently they were arguing over who would get the best places in this new kingdom of God. At the same time they were seemingly accepting the soon to be death of Jesus. They were almost vying over who would be the most loyal. Jesus had the Apostles and disciples prepare for the Passover on Thursday the day before the Passover was normally celebrated. The huge crowds made it impossible for everyone to celebrate the Passover on Friday, so Jews from distant places were allowed to celebrate it the day before. It was this circumstance that allowed the true Paschal Lamb to die on Friday, the feast of Passover, and wipe away the sins of all mankind. The Passover meal was celebrated in a very solemn manner, as everything was done according to the instructions of Moses, during the meal. The participants ate standing with a walking stick in their hands as if they were going on a journey. The bread was unleavened as the Israelites left so quickly that they had no time to leaven the bread. The doorposts were sprinkled with blood to identify the household as that of the Israelites so that the destroying angel would pass over the house. During the meal Jesus would pause and use the moment to teach his Apostles some truth. But then, ever aware of what would happen, he said that someone at the table would betray him. This thought must have cut very deeply into the heart of Jesus. These were the ones who had been with him from the beginning and they had seen all that Jesus did and he surely loved everyone of them dearly even the one who would betray him. An episode at the table illustrates that Jesus knew who it was that would betray him. In spite of this, Jesus did not disclose Judas to the rest of the Apostles. There is a lesson here for each of us. There are times when we are betrayed, so to speak, in relatively small matters and how do we react. Certainly not like Jesus did. We want to strike back. Instead, we should show compassion and forgive in our hearts and offer it up to the Lord who surely suffered much more than we ever will. After the supper, Jesus took a towel and a pitcher of water and proceeded to wash the feet of the twelve Apostles. What a great act of humility. Here is the Son of God, creator of the Universe including all mankind, kneeling down and washing the feet of his creation. The Church reenacts this event during Holy Week every year to teach us to be humble just as Jesus was. Today everyone wants to be successful and have everyone look up to them. No one wants to do the every day dirty jobs. We want to be important. Jesus teaches us here that it is better to be a servant doing God's will than a big shot doing his own will. After the fall of Adam and Eve, God began to become more and more distant from mankind due to the increasing sinfulness of the human race. It became so bad, that only eight persons and the animals in an ark were saved by a huge flood that covered the earth. Afterwards God promised never to do this again. In spite of that, man increased in sinfulness even to this present day. God was seen as some distant person in a place called heaven far away. Men tried to bring God closer by making and worshipping wooden or metal idols. Some men saw in the sun and moon a god to worship. Although the Jews worshipped the true God, they fell into idolatry and sinfulness. So, God came down personally in the form of his only Son to reveal himself to us. After the great sacrifice of Jesus on the cross and his resurrection, Jesus would return to his heavenly Father. What would he leave us? After washing their feet, Jesus impressed on the Apostles the signification of what he had done and told them that they must act in the same manner to others. He again spoke of his approaching death and how they would flee, but that after he rose they would understand what he had accomplished. Then Jesus did something that was unheard of and would be hard for many to accept. When he would go heaven, he would come back to everyone personally through his Church. Jesus took bread and said, "This is my Body." He took a cup of wine and said," This is my Blood. Do this in remembrance of me." In the Catholic Church when the priest says these words, then the bread is changed into the Body of Jesus and the wine into the Blood of Jesus. When we eat this bread, we are really eating the Body of Jesus and when we drink this wine we are really drinking the blood of Jesus. The bread and wine seem unchanged, but the substance has changed. We believe this through faith in the words of Jesus who is truth himself. What a wonderful gift God has given us through his Son, Jesus. There are many ways to look at this. Jesus is the Word of God. When he enters into us through the Eucharist, we have the Word of God within us. Being free of sin, this Word of God can become our word which we can put into action. When we receive Jesus in the Eucharist, then Jesus the King of Heaven and Earth is within us and we become a part of the kingdom of God; Just as Jesus said the Kingdom of God is within you. Wherever God is, there is his Kingdom whither in Heaven or here on Earth. Jesus said that the Father and He are One. Since there is only one God, then the Holy Spirit is also in both the Father and the Son. How can this be? I don't know and neither do you. It's a mystery. We accept it on faith because Jesus said so. When we receive the Eucharist, then we receive not only Jesus in his humanity and divinity, but also the Father and the Holy Spirit, because they are inseparable. Never in the history of mankind has God been so close to his people as today. How thankful we should be. Just think. When we pray we know that God hears all prayers and will do what is best for us. When we receive Jesus in the Eucharist, we can talk personally to God because he is within us. What a great time to knock on the doors of heaven and know they're open and God is there listening to us in the depths of our heart. There is no doubt that in the Catholic Church this act of bringing Jesus present to us in the form of bread and wine is the core of our faith. We believe this act takes place because the Church teaches it. Jesus did not write anything. He taught his followers orally. The Apostles handed down the teachings of Jesus orally and it was not until the middle of the fourth century that the books we know as the Bible, the Old and New Testaments, were put together and accepted by all Christians. The Gospel accounts in the Bible do not contradict the Catholic Mass and the teachings of the Church. Rather they reinforce the Church's teachings. Jesus said several times that it was necessary for one to eat his Body and drink his Blood to have everlasting life. When people walked away including some of his disciples, Jesus asked the Apostles if they would leave also. In other words, Jesus meant literally what he said no matter who would not accept this teaching of his. It was only at the Last Supper that the method that Jesus would employ to allow people to eat his Flesh and drink his Blood was revealed. St. Paul in his letters emphasized the importance of this mystery. The veneration of the Blessed Virgin Mary, the authority of the Pope, and the Eucharist are the main targets of attack by the enemies of the Catholic Church. The greatest attacks center on the Eucharist because the Eucharist is the lifeblood of the Church. It is not a play. It is the sacrifice of Jesus brought forward and presented to the faithful. Time means nothing to God. We are there with Jesus on our altar through the action of the priest. How many of us as we approach communion realize that the God of Heaven and Earth is waiting for us to receive him. Do we really approach Jesus with reverence and adoration? Are our minds and hearts waiting in anticipation of this great moment when Jesus will be present to us, Body and Blood, in the very depths of our body? If in the past we did not appreciate this great gift that God has given us, then we need to change our attitude. We need to pray that we will not receive the Body and Blood of Jesus in an unworthy manner. When Jesus is present in the consecrated hosts, he is completely defenseless. There have been many many times through the ages when Jesus, present in the host, has been mistreated, tossed aside, and even have had knives pierce the hosts. These many instances of mistreatment show how much love Jesus has for us that he was willing to accept this mistreatment when he gave us the Eucharist. While no amount of reparation could possibly make up for this mistreatment of Jesus, we should offer up our prayers of reparation and sacrifice for these outrages. And like Jesus we should offer prayers for those who commit these outrages. We did not live and were not present when Jesus walked and taught his message. He is present in the Eucharist and we can visit Jesus in the tabernacle and spend some time praying and meditating on the great works that he accomplished for us. Were it not for God, we would not have life. All the things that we have accomplished would not have been possible were it not for God. Our world, and all that is in it, is there because God created it. The beauty of the world that you see at this very moment is there because God created it especially for you to enjoy at this very moment. Do we show God the gratitude that we owe him? We can bring all our joys and sorrows to Jesus as he wants to hear them from us even though he is fully aware of them. He wishes to comfort us in our hour of need. Our prayers are always answered although not always the way we would like. That's because Jesus wants what is best for us to attain eternal life in the next world. Many of us are able to attend a service where the Blessed Sacrament is exposed. There is Jesus in the host on the altar looking out to see who bothered to come and see him. What a great moment to pray and show our adoration to God for all that he has done for us. Even just to sit and keep him company is surely a great blessing for us. We must keep in mind that we are Catholics because we know that God is present and within us through this great sacrament of Holy Eucharist. This is where Jesus is always present, ready to help us through whatever problems we may have. He wishes to share our joys. This is our lifeline to God. This is what unites us to the Body of Christ, the Church.

AGONY

*A*nd they came to a farm call Gethsemani. And he saith to his disciples: Sit you here, while I pray. And he taketh Peter and James and John with him: and he began to fear and to be heavy. And he saith to them: My soul is sorrowful even unto death. Stay you here and watch. And when he was gone forward a little, he fell flat on the ground: and he prayed that, if it might be, the hour might pass from him. And he saith: Abba, Father, all things are possible to thee: remove this chalice from me: but not what I will, but what thou wilt. And he cometh and findeth them sleeping. And he saith to Peter: Simon, sleepest thou? Couldst thou not watch one hour? Watch ye: and pray that you enter not into temptation. The spirit indeed is willing, but the flesh is weak. And going away again, he prayed, saying the same words. And when he returned, he found them again asleep (for their eyes were heavy): and they knew not what to answer him. And he cometh the third time and saith to them: Sleep ye now and take your rest. It is enough. The hour is come: behold the Son of man shall be betrayed into the hands *of sinners. Rise up: let us go. Behold, he that will betray me is at hand. (MK 14: 32-42)*

This meditation would be incomplete unless we answered some basic questions. Why did Jesus have to suffer and die? Isn't there a better way to reconcile God and mankind? Couldn't just one drop of the blood of Jesus do the job of redemption? There is a vast difference between God and us, so much so that we can't always completely understand the actions of God. With our God given intelligence we will try to answer the above questions. God is pure spirit and we are created beings as is everything in the universe. We cannot know anything about God as a result unless he chooses to reveal it to us. Our life, intelligence, free will, and everything that we are able to do is a gift from God. When Adam and Eve sinned and the human race that followed sinned, then we all lost the good life God had wanted for us and most important of all we lost the friendship of God. When one of us harms another, there is always a way to make restitution for the harm and injury done. When God is injured there is no way to make restitution for the sin or sins committed because God needs nothing and has everything. Indeed, God is perfect. Only another divine person such as God could make restitution. The second Person in God wanted to make restitution and so he became human like us while still retaining his divinity. Thus, God the Son would be able to make restitution as he is equal in all respects to God the Father. But what can humanity offer as it would have to be the greatest gift that mankind possess. The greatest gift we have is the gift of the God-man, Jesus. The greatest gift of anyone is the gift of life. Throughout the ages, men have offered the best of their crops or animals to God by burning them completely so that they would not have them anymore. A sacrifice of their goods to God. So, Jesus would have to give his life to God by dying. Could not Jesus have died in a lesser manner? Remember Jesus told us to be afraid of the second death, the death of our soul. Why? Because that is an eternal dying with pain in the fires of hell. Jesus had to suffer such a death though not eternal as God shows us what the effects of sin really are. And only God can judge what is necessary to satisfy his Divine Justice. Before we begin our meditation on the agony of Jesus, it is necessary for us to understand the essential difference between Jesus as man and the rest of us. Jesus had two natures, human and divine even though he was one person. In his human nature Jesus was just like Adam and Eve before the fall. He possessed the preternatural gift of integrity. There was complete harmony between the spirit and flesh. The human passions or bodily appetites were completely controlled by the will and reason. Consequently Jesus had no inclination to evil. Also, Jesus would feel not only physical and mental suffering as we do, but he would feel these sufferings deep within his soul or spirit. It would be like someone scolding us unjustly and our soul would feel like someone had slapped us in the interior of our body. Jesus arrives at the garden of Gethsemani with his Apostles to begin his final preparation for his supreme act of redemption. He leaves all the Apostles except Peter, James, and John at the entrance and proceeds further into the garden. The three Apostles are told to watch and pray while Jesus goes further into the garden to pray to his heavenly Father. Jesus was about to make the most dangerous and important decision of his life. His first action was to kneel down and pray to his heavenly Father. How many times do we make important decisions in our life and we never give a thought about asking God to help guide us to a right decision. If we bring God into our important decision making process, we surely can be more successful. Bringing God along on our everyday life is a sure road to the only success that really counts: everlasting life. Jesus is sad and sorrowful as he not only realizes the terrible sufferings he is about to undergo, but also the reasons that made his sacrificial offering necessary, the sins of all mankind. Jesus in a certain manner caused his Divinity to return into the most Holy Trinity. Jesus did this out of infinite love so that his humanity supported by the love of his human heart alone would endure the suffering necessary for our eternal salvation. To fully atone for all the sins of the world from the sin of Adam and Eve to the end of the world, these sins had to be presented to Jesus in all their ugliness which Satan was only too happy to do. Satan, of course, was fully unaware that Jesus was God, the second Person of the Trinity. How Jesus suffered as each sin was shown. Was Jesus really ready to suffer for such as this? My sins in all their terribleness were displayed. Oh! That I could find a hole to hide in away from Jesus. So greatly am I ashamed of these sins which caused Jesus to suffer so much. How much love Jesus has to take us back to him in total forgiveness. Jesus took upon himself not only the sins of those who would be converted, but also those who would die unrepentant. Satan was not just content with showing all the sins of everyone; he also accused Jesus of sinning himself by the various actions Jesus did. Why not cure this person? You caused this person to sin. You didn't help this one. You spent money given you for yourself, etc.

Satan, the master of deceit tried what he could to discourage Jesus from making his great sacrifice. When we look at the immensity of the sins committed it does not effect us as much as it did Jesus who realizes the great effrontery it causes to almighty God. In relying on the weakness of his human nature, sinless though he was, Jesus must have shuddered at the thought of death. But it was his Father's will that was to be done, not his own. The first part of the agony of Jesus, Satan showed Jesus the immensity of the debt that Jesus was about to assume. In the second part, there was displayed to Jesus in the greatest detail, the suffering necessary to discharge this immense debt to God. Satan did not know that expiation of all these sins is possible. Jesus now saw all the future sufferings of his Apostles, disciples, friends, and the followers of his Church. He saw the terrible persecutions that takes place to the end of the world. He saw the tortures and deaths of so many of his followers. He saw his Church torn apart by schisms and heresies. Many Christians refuse to follow the teachings of his Church and draw many persons away from his Church. Then, there were the very many persons who stayed in the Church, but taught false ideas of his teachings. Many clergy caused great scandals among the innocent and faithful Catholics. There were so many people for whom his sacrifice would be in vain. The great gift that he gave of his Body and Blood in the Eucharist would be violated and profaned. Many persons would deny his teachings given by his beloved Church. The Blessed Sacrament would be discarded or violated. Many persons would ignore his presence. Many priests would celebrate the Mass carelessly and would act in an irreverent manner toward the Eucharist. This great gift that Jesus gave to all humans would be in many cases not given the recognition it deserved. How many times have we been guilty of not fully realizing this great gift that Jesus has left us. He is there present on our altars awaiting for us to greet him with love and thanksgiving. Do we really comprehend the immense amount of suffering that Jesus underwent in order to bring us into friendship with God? We owe him so much and we show so little gratitude. Let us resolve to do a better job of showing our love for Jesus in the most Blessed Sacrament where he is present. Not only that, but Jesus comes into our very heart at Holy Communion. We can talk to the actual presence of our Lord and Savior. How Jesus must have suffered from the ingratitude of the whole human race and realize that his sufferings for so many would be in vain. Consider how we should act and kneel in thanksgiving for the great love that Jesus has for each and every one of us. There is a natural repugnance to suffer and this would be true for Jesus also. How Jesus could conquer this natural repugnance to suffer is beyond our understanding. It has our great admiration. Jesus would now be shown the good results of his sufferings. The release from limbo of the many good people who could not go to heaven until the doors were opened by Jesus. The love that so many had for God. Then, of course, there was the future saints led by the Blessed Virgin Mary. Saints that suffered torture and death rather than deny Christ. The holy army of the blessed that remained ever faithful to Jesus and his Church. Jesus loved us so much that he would have suffered even if it was for just one soul. Finally, Jesus was shown the future scenes of his passion and death. If the Son of God was to die, he would need to see what the future would be like. So, the terrible passion in all its cruelty and torture, mockery, scourging, and crucifixion was displayed so that Jesus knew exactly what he would be suffering. It would be his final act of obedience to his heavenly Father. We can not fully comprehend the full extent of the sufferings that Jesus endured during his agony in the garden. It should be noted that he went three times to his three Apostles to ask them to watch and pray with him. Jesus undoubtedly felt all alone at this time and it's no wonder. The temptations to just forget the whole thing was there. But Jesus was ever mindful of the will of his Heavenly Father. This is divine love. This is what love is all about. How sad that we have such a hard time imitating Jesus. We will never really get close to God unless we meditate from time to time on the passion and death of Jesus. This is really the greatest love story in the world. To ransom us from death, God gave up the greatest treasure he had, his only Son to a horrible death. A death that his Son willingly accepted not only because the Father willed it, but also because the Son loved us just as much as the Father. In conclusion, if we love God we will show our love by obeying his commandments and living a life worthy of God. There is no greater love than to give up our life for another person.

SCOURGING

A *nd Pilate seeing that he prevailed nothing, but that rather a tumult was made, taking water washed his hands before the people, saying: I am innocent of the blood of this just man. Look you to it. And the whole people answering, said: His blood be upon us and upon our children. Then he released to them Barabbas: and having scourged Jesus, delivered him unto them to be crucified. (MT 27:24-26)*

Before we meditate on the physical sufferings of Jesus, we need to consider why this suffering was necessary. From a human standpoint, all this suffering seems unnecessary and cruel. How can any father subject his son to all this suffering? However, what we are dealing with is not just the life on this earth, but our future life as well. Through original sin man lost the perfect life with God in Paradise. Not only that, but man chose to serve Satan rather than God. Through the centuries mankind piled up sin after sin not only against God, but also against man's fellow creatures made in the image of God. Now how is it possible to make amends to God for all the injuries, that is sins, that we committed. What is the proper restitution that a person can give to God to make everything right? Only a person equal to God could give the proper restitution to God. Although there is only one God, there are three Persons in the one God as Jesus revealed to us. But this restitution has to come from a human being. Thus it was that the Son of God, Jesus, became a man to make this restitution. Who can determine what Jesus, the Son of Man, must do to set things right? Only God knows what will satisify his Divine Justice. What about God's Divine Mercy? After God's Divine Justice is satisified, then God gives us his Divine Mercy through his Son, Jesus, who accomplished the reconcilation. Jesus gives us this Divine Mercy through his Church which dispenses whatever graces are needed. As we meditate on the terrible sufferings that Jesus underwent, it is good to remember that it was necessary to satisfy the Divine Justice of God. If not, it would never have happened. Our sins are directly responsible for these sufferings that Jesus underwent. Every time we sin, we contributed to the sufferings of Jesus. Let us begin our meditation by examining what led up to the scourging of Jesus. The betrayal of Jesus by Judas was not a surprise to Jesus, but it was a very sad moment. The betrayal of Jesus by one of his own Apostles and that by a kiss hurt Jesus very much. It is not unique in history and Jesus surely offered his betrayal in reparation for all the many betrayals that take place here among men. We need to resolve never to let money attract us to such an extent that we would betray one of our friends. On the way to the midnight tribunal, Jesus suffers blows and other outrages that happen to persons judged to be common criminals. He offers his sufferings silently for all those who wind up in similar situations. Jesus is condemned by false witnesses at an illegal trial. This is not unlike many trials that happen throughout history and even happen in this present day. Many unfortunate persons endure the same injustice as Jesus. Jesus bears all this outrage in silence and prayer. He offers it up for those in like circumstances. The daytime trial results in the same verdict for Jesus as he endures further blows and insults. No one is brought in who has listened to Jesus throughout his career except his enemies. There is no one at this sham trial to represent Jesus. Oh! How terrible are the sins that we mortal men commit to subject our gentle Jesus to so much suffering. Apparently the Jewish leaders could not put a person to death, although they were apparently ready to do so for a woman caught in adultery. What better way to completely humiliate Jesus then to have the Romans crucify him among a group of criminals. So to Pontius Pilate, Jesus was brought to be excuted. The Roman Governor, Pontius Pilate, was not so accommodating. He was going to examine Jesus to see if he was guilty of any criminal action. He found Jesus innocent. The Jewish leaders and the mob they had gathered were furious. Then Pilate had an idea. He would get rid of this problem and send Jesus to Herod for judgment. Jesus was then dragged over to King Herod for judgment. At first the King was happy to see Jesus and puffed up because Pilate had sent Jesus over to him. Herod cared nothing for the accusations, he wanted Jesus to perform a miracle for him. Jesus was silent before this pathetic ruler. Herod became mad at the silence of Jesus and he made a fool of Jesus. Here is our beloved Lord subjected to the worst insults and paraded around as a fool What love Jesus has for us to endure all this in order to make reparation for our sins that we so many times lightly commit. We should throw ourselves down on the ground and ask for a mercy we don't deserve. Jesus is now back at Pilate's palace. Herod has found nothing, so Pilate can release him. But the Jewish leaders and the mob object. A riot may ensue. Then Pilate offers them a choice. Who shall he release: Jesus or a terrible criminal and murderer named Barabbas. Barabbas is freed. How many times has this happened that criminals are set free while the innocent are punished. Jesus willingly suffers this indignity for the sake of all those innocents who have suffered. Thus far Jesus has suffered so much for our sins, but it is not enough. Oh! That I could take back every single one of the many sins that I committed. Pilate cannot allow Jesus to go free. There may be riots. Pilate could lose his job or even his life. Pilate does not know the words of Jesus: "What does it profit a man to gain the whole world and suffer the loss of his soul?" Pilate then decides to chastise Jesus and then let him go. The chastisement of the Romans was a terrible scourging by cruel soldiers who generally considered the prisoner an enemy of the state. There were times when criminals were scourged to death and Jesus could expect to find no pity from these executioners. The intruments used in the scourging were different and few, but very deadly. Some rods consisted of flexible white wood or strips of hard leather. There were rough rods with thorns, knots, and splinters. The worst rods were whips made of chains or straps with iron points or hooks that would tear off whole pieces of skin and flesh. Jesus was stripped of his clothing and tightly bound to the whipping pillar so that he could not move or defend himself. Then the horrible scourging took place. There was no sound part of the body of Jesus that was not hit. And when they finished with one side, they turned Jesus over to beat him on the other side and his face was not spared. No words could do justice to describe this terrible scene. We cannot describe it further. The horror of the scene just described should impress us with the horror of sin committed against God. There is no other reason for it. God would never have allowed it to happen unless it was necessary. It is necessary to demonstrate to all of us the immensity of the sins that we have committed. Not only does this terrible suffering and death of Jesus restore our friendship with God, but we have by the mercy of God been admitted to heaven as adopted sons and daughters of God. What sins does this scourging wipe away. There are two types of sins that come to mind: Pride and Immorality. Pride leads us to consider ourselves entitled to do whatever we want whether God likes it or not. Immorality especially sins of a sexual nature drive man to act like animals and not like the image and likeness of God that every person has.. There are so many sins of pride that can be committed and we are all certainly guilty of committing pride in some degree or another. We don't listen to authority placed over us because we know better. As children we may at times have decided that we can do something harmful to us because we know better than parents or adults. Rules are made for others not us. I am more important than those other people because I'm smarter. Pride can take so many forms that we have to be so careful. We need to overcome our tendency to Pride with the humility that we see in the suffering Jesus. God though he was, he offered himself up for you and me. Jesus gained nothing for himself personally because he is perfect. What he did do was show his love for us. He gave us a means to enter heaven with him in the next life and the means to escape the second death, hell. The Blessed Virgin Mary said at Fatima that more souls go to hell because of sexual sins than for any other reason. Why is this? Because it is so easy to indulge our sexual desires unless we acquire discipline. Prayer and the grace of God can go a long way to help us avoid these types of sins. Sexual sins combine pride with disobedience to lead us away from the plan that God had for a man and a woman. The greatest gift that God has is the ability to create. We see it all around us. God's greatest creation was to create Adam and Eve in his image and likeness. God gave mankind this greatest gift to procreate just as he did in creating the first man and woman. Sexual sins are the misuse of the greatest gift that we have been given. Man and woman were meant to have children and to raise them up to recognize God. Any use of this great gift of God for any other purpose is a sin. Any one with a clear eye can see the terrible effects of this on society today. The human race was meant to be united under God obeying the laws of nature that God created. The free will that we were given was meant for us to do good. Now those who follow Jesus are a part of a body of his followers. We call this the Body of Christ with Jesus as our head and leader. Jesus shows us in this scourging what this body looks like when it embraces sin. This meditation should make us resolve to follow Jesus by being obedient to the laws and commandments of God and his Church.

CROWNING

*T*hen the soldiers of the governor, taking Jesus into
the hall, gathered together unto him the whole
band. And stripping him, they put a scarlet cloak about
him. And plattig a crown of thorns, they put upon it upon
his head, and a reed in his right hand. And bowing the
knee before him, they mocked him, saying: Hail, King of
the Jews. And spitting upon him, they took the reed and
struck his head. And after they had mocked him, they took
off the cloak from him and put on him his own garments
and led him away to crucify him. (MT 27:27-31)

From the earliest times, it has been the custom to
place a crown upon the head of champions and famous
people. Kings were generally crowned with elaborate
golden crowns. Many were adorned with many precious
jewels. One could look at that person and know that that
was a very important person deserving of a great deal
of respect. Subjects of kings were expected to kneel
before the king and pay the utmost respect to their ruler.
Anyone not showing respect would be promptly arrested
and thrown in prison. The Roman soldiers having been

stationed in Judaea for quite some time were probably well aware of the Jewish prophet that some say was the messiah, the future king of the Jews. The Romans held the Jewish population in contempt as a backward people. They also may have been bribed by the Jewish leaders to mistreat Jesus. After the brutal scourging, Jesus was brought to a stool with broken pottery on it and roughly seated. The horribly disfigured Jesus should have been shown some sympathy by the soldiers. These soldiers were hardened by cruelty and a life of sin. There was no mercy shown to Jesus. Instead, Jesus was treated as a joke in the cruelest possible manner. This is a lesson for us in that if we allow ourselves to lead a life of sin, then we too can become hardened to where we show no mercy toward others. This would lead us to a life without respect for life or the welfare of others. One soldier makes a crown of thorns to crown the make believe king. One tradition says there were 96 thorns that pierced the head of Jesus. To make sure the crown would stay on and to inflict as much pain as possible, the crown was pounded on the head of Jesus. There is no migraine headache that can compare to the pain that Jesus felt. A dirty red robe was then placed on Jesus to mock him as king. To us it is a real symbol of the first martyr for our salvation. Kings usually have a golden scepter to show their authority to rule. Jesus is given a hollow reed. Then the soldiers knelt and paid fake homage to Jesus. They blindfold Jesus, slap him in the face, and ask him to predict who did it, all the time laughing and joking. The scene is one to make a true Christian cry. The Lord of heaven and earth having been treated like that. Our God, the second Person of the Blessed Trinity, held in scorn. How could God allow his Son to be treated this way? It is necessary to satisfy the Divine Justice or it would not have happened. Oh! How terrible are the sins that you and I commit. There is a great importance to be learned from this mystery. Every thought and action that we do has its beginning in the brain. Our brain controls our will and can overcome our emotions. The good that we do begins there. Likewise, the evil that we conceive or do has its origins in the brain. The sufferings of Jesus during the crowning of the thorns is to make reparation for all the sins that originate in our mind or brain. A person who is alive but whose brain does not function is in a vegetative state. That person is unable to do anything and has to have someone else take care of him. It is the brain that controls all our thoughts and actions. If we wish to follow Christ, then we need to carefully cultivate our mind to the things that matter the most in life. Nothing is more important to us then to live a life that will enable us to reach heaven in the next life after our death. How often have we imitated the Roman guards in making fun of others? Did we do so in a cruel or malicious manner? Have we looked down upon other people because of their race, their religion, or their background? Have we made fun of them openly and maliciously? They were created just like us in the image and likeness of God. No matter what faults or evil actions they may have done, they are our brothers and sisters. The mind of man is a marvelous thing and is capable of creating wonders and solving great mysteries. It is also capable of creating evil in so many forms. Today we can see this in the internet, movies, books, and television. The great tragedy is that a single book for example which causes one to sin can last for many many years and affect many many people. A sin like that can take on a life of its own. Is it any wonder then that Jesus had to suffer the crowning of his head by thorns to make satisfaction for these sins. No one knows what goes on in the mind of another person. The mind can hide a million thoughts. Many of these can be sinful and are known only to God. We like to think that nobody knows, but God does. We need to stop any sinful thoughts that we have and find something to take their place. God has given us a beautiful mind and we need to fill that mind with beautiful thoughts. Any problems we have can be solved by recourse to prayer. This mystery reminds us of the great power and authority that many people are given in this world. Just think how this power and authority has been misused throughout the centuries by kings and other governments. In our own times we have seen this happen also. If we exercise any power or authority over anyone, we need to ensure that we are doing so in a Christian manner. Otherwise we are merely adding to the sufferings of Jesus. We need to remember that Jesus, because his soul is intimately connected to his body, suffers as well in his interior. The insults and blasphemous words echo and reechoes throughout his body as though they were many darts piercing his very soul. The tongue of a person can be the workshop of the devil or it can be the workshop of an angel. So much damage can be done to so many by so few words. All around us we are bombarded by words that we need to keep out of our vocabulary. It is not easy, but we must persevere to eliminate the sinful words and build up the good words. Once again the best solution is prayer. God has given us twenty four hours each day to do whatever we want to do. Our life should include some of that time devoted to God who after all has given us life without which we would not exist. On rising in the morning, we need to think of Jesus and what he did for us and say a little prayer. We should do this at noon, in the evening, and at nighttime. Each meal should be started with a prayer of thanksgiving. An hour a day is little enough to return to God in prayer. Recourse to one of the many devotions that the Church offers is little enough to offer God. Love is a much misused word today as most people consider it an emotion. It is rather an act of the will. Jesus shows us true love through the act of his will during his passion. When you meditate on this mystery think of the love Jesus has for you to undergo these sufferings. Jesus shows his love for us through the act of his will that he accomplished. Love is wanting the greatest good for the one that is loved. Our greatest good and goal is heaven. When you think of the many sufferings that Jesus undergoes in this mystery, think of the love that accompanies these sufferings. They are for you. They have opened the gates of heaven for you. They have made you the intimate friend of God. They allow you to share in his divinity. The only thing left is your choice. What is it to be? You don't just have the natural law to guide you anymore. You have the teaching of Jesus. You don't need to wonder if you have the correct interpretation of the teaching of Jesus because he gave you the Church to guide you. The sufferings of Jesus are calling you to a far better life than you can ever have now here on earth. If you are ever in a position where you are mocked or persecuted, remember what Jesus went through for you so that you can obtain everlasting life in the world to come. Remember that Jesus loves you. Even now Jesus is lovingly watching you and waiting for you to join him in Heaven. The decision is yours!

JOURNEY

A nd from henceforth Pilate sought to release him.
*But the Jews cried out saying: If thou release this
man, thou art not Caesar's friend. For whosoever maketh
himself a king speaketh against Caesar. Now when Pilate
had heard these words, he brought Jesus forth and sat
down in the judgment seat, in the place that is called
Lithostrotos, and in Hebrew Gabbatha. And it was the
parasceve of the pasch, about the sixth hour: and he
saith to the Jews: Behold your king. But they cried out:
Away with him: Crucify him. Pilate saith to them: Shall
I crucify your king? The chief priests answered: We have
no king but Caesar. Then therefore he delivered him to
them to be crucified. And they took Jesus and led him
forth. And bearing his own cross, he went forth to the
place which is called Calvary, but in Hebrew Golgotha.
(JN 19:12-17)*

Pilate knew that Jesus was an innocent person and
not guilty of any crime. When the crowd set Barabbus
free instead of Jesus, Pilate said he would scourge Jesus
and set him free. After the scourging and crowning with

thorns, Jesus appears clothed with an old red cloak, bleeding, flesh torn from head to foot, and unrecognizable to everyone. Pilate tells the crowd: Ecce homo! Behold the man! Instead of sympathy which this picture of Jesus should have generated, the crowd cries: Crucify him! It is close to a riot. Pilate gives in, but he tries to exonerate himself by washing his hands and saying that he is innocent of killing this innocent person. How many times in this world of ours have we seen innocent people suffer because of weak or wicked judges or lawyers. Jesus here offers up his unjust sentence for all the times that innocent people have been unjustly condemned to prison or executed. We need to make sure that we do not become like the mob in taking vengeance on persons who may well be innocent. Jesus now takes up his cross. He embraces it as one would embrace a loved one. How very different from us. We shy away from our crosses or complain or run away. We just don't want to follow Jesus. It's too hard. We won't let the Holy Spirit help us in our trials. We would rather complain. As Jesus begins the short journey to Calvary, he is so weakened from all the punishment that he has undergone that he does not go very far before he collapses under his cross with his first great fall. Most of us do not remember the first time that we sinned. For us it was indeed a great fall. We failed God who has done so much for us. It is the first step toward losing our friendship with God. Let us pray that we don't take the first step toward embracing a life of sin and a loss of friendship with God.. The journey of Jesus takes him face to face with his beloved mother, Mary. At the actual sight of Jesus, she experienced first hand the terrible punishment inflicted on Jesus and her soul recoils as if a sharp knife had entered in. Jesus likewise suffered to see his mother suffer so much at the sight of him. This is what sin causes. It spreads so that it hurts not just one person but also all those who are united to that person. It is not another person's sins that we should consider but our own. We are all guilty. We need to erase our sins through confession and pray constantly for forgiveness and perseverance in avoiding all sin. The Blessed Virgin Mary, because of her union with the sufferings of her son, is in a unique position to help us on our pilgrimage here on earth. God has sent her many times to help us to avoid sin and to receive the graces that Jesus can send us. We need to have a close relationship with Mary as she is there always ready to help us through her Son. As Jesus goes on, it becomes apparent that the beatings that he had taken had weakened him to the point that he would never make it to the hill of Calvary. So the Roman soldiers grabbed a pagan man and forced him to assist Jesus in carrying his cross. It is easy to imagine how angry Simon was when he was forced to help Jesus especially when it was apparent that he would have to carry most of the weight.. Isn't that just like us when we are forced to do a good deed or to do something that we know we should, but we really don't want to. Just maybe like Simon, we may be helping God himself by our actions. We need not look for a reward as our love for Jesus should be reward enough. Notice the attitude of Simon as he notices the patience and resignation of Jesus. He begins to be pleased to be able to assist Jesus. Isn't that what we should do to our fellow brothers and sisters. There is a great need in this world for more persons like Simon. We can be one of those persons. We too need to look at the pain and sufferings of Jesus to realize the enormity of our sins and offenses. Let us be like Jesus and bear the burdens of life without complaint and happy to help our fellow man. Just like Jesus would want us to do. Throughout the entire passion of Jesus, no one lifted one finger to help Jesus. Jesus was all alone and solitary in his sufferings. Suddenly this changed as a woman named Seraphia came forward to Jesus and presented her veil to wipe the face of Jesus. Jesus took the veil and wiped his face. He gave it back to her with thanks. Running back to her room, she knelt down. It was then that she noticed the bloody face of Jesus with wonderful distinctness impressed on her veil, Because of her action, she received the name of Veronica meaning vera (true) and icon (picture or image).We too can be capable of brave actions like that of Veronica if we perse-vere in prayer and take part in the various acts of spiri-tual and corporal works of mercy. Prayer coupled with fasting and almsgiving can change us into courageous saints. By this time in spite of the help of Simon, Jesus has his second great fall and would seem to be unable to continue. So many times even when we are helped by others we feel that we cannot continue. We are ready to give up. We find that we cannot overcome a bad addic-tion to some sin and we fall a second or more times. We want to quit trying. Quitting an addiction is never easy and we may have this problem late into our life. Our prayers don't seem to help. We get discouraged and even despondent. We just can't quit no matter how many times we try. God seems so far away, but he is there. He wants us to keep trying. Keep praying. Keep up hope. Go to confession and the Eucharist. Pray daily. You will be triumphant in the end. God promises you. And Jesus rises after his second fall. He has a mission to save you and me. Only he can do this. At the outskirts of Jerusalem,

Jesus is met by a wailing crowd of women who had been helped by him. They were crying over the sad state of affairs that had happened to Jesus. Jesus could have wallowed in their sympathy and joined with them bewailing his tragic state of affairs. He didn't. Jesus tells them to weep for themselves and their children. In veiled words he is prophesying the terrible destruction that will take place in Judea by the Romans in just under 50 years. Even toward the end, Jesus is more concerned about others than he is about himself. It is after all the reason he came on earth- to redeem the human race. The single minded purpose of Jesus is to reach the cross and to die. His sole concern is to save souls. This is his great love. This is divine love. We cannot equal it, but we can try to imitate it in our daily lives. This is a love not based on emotion and feelings, but on the will. Is it true love to discard a person when that person grows old and loses its outer beauty? No. True love is faithful through thick and thin. No matter what happens, a person shows true love by always being faithful. This is what Jesus did. He did not let anything deter him from his mission of redemption because he loves us. Can we really do less? Just before his journey to Calvary is ended, Jesus experiences his third great fall. The beatings, the loss of blood, the lack of water, and the constant pain that will not go away cause Jesus to fall again. He is beaten and prodded to get up. Jesus finally rises to meet his final sufferings. Many times we feel that we cannot go on. It's just too much for us. We want an easy way out. Yet when we look at Jesus we see that he did not look for or take an easy way out. All our life Jesus was with us and the times were good. We were happy and enjoying life. God was good to us. Then suddenly things seem to change. Things aren't so good any more. Some of us are close to despair. Why doesn't God help us we cry out. God will always help us in the life that truly matters, the life that we will lead after death. You can count on it. All human beings were given free will to do good. But they are not prevented from doing evil because they are not robots. They have the same freedom that God has. Only God is all goodness so that he can't do anything against himself. So men do evil things and evil things happen to good people. But our ultimate life is our second life. The life that we will live after our death. This is the life that God will make sure that everyone who truly loves him and remains faithful to him will enjoy. We know this because he promised it and because God is all goodness and keeps his promises. So Jesus shows us that this journey of ours is not always an easy one. But like Jesus we can come through it if we remain faithful to his commandments to love God and our neighbor.

CRUCIFIXION

*A*nd when they were come to the place which is called Calvary, they crucified him there: and the robbers, one on the right hand, and the other on the left. And Jesus said: Father, forgive them, for they know not what they do. But they, dividing his garments, cast lots. And the people stood beholding. And the rulers with them derided him, saying: He saved others: let him save himself, if he be the Christ, the elect of God. And the soldiers also mocked him, coming to him and offering him vinegar. And saying: If thou be the king of the Jews, save thyself. And there was also a superscription written over him in letters of Greek and Latin and Hebrew THIS IS THE KING OF THE JEWS. And one of those robbers who were hanged blasphemed him, saying: If thou be Christ, save thyself and us. But the other answering, rebuked him, saying: Neither dost thou fear God, seeing thou art under the same condemnation? And we indeed justly: for we receive the due reward of our deeds. But this man hath done no evil. And he said to Jesus: Lord, remember me when thou shalt come into thy kingdom. And Jesus said to him:

Amen I say to thee: This day thou shalt be with me in paradise. And it was almost the sixth hour: and there was darkness over all the earth until the ninth hour. And the sun was darkened, and the veil of the temple was rent in the midst. And Jesus crying with a loud voice, said: Father, into thy hands I commend my spirit. And saying this, he gave up the ghost. (LK 23:33-46)

Our beloved Savior Jesus arrived at the place of crucifixion with his exhausted body torn and bleeding. He had scarcely a moment's rest when his executioners came and tore off his clothes from his body. This caused further pain as they had adhered to his body. The seamless robe Mary had made for him could not be removed because of the crown of thorns. So they took the crown of thorns off and after removing the robe placed the crown of thorns back on his head. Jesus was naked and would have been crucified that way had not a bystander given him a cloth to cover himself. Jesus stood there silent and meek as a lamb without complaint. Up to this point, we can hardly continue our meditation. The love that Jesus is showing in reparation for all our sins makes us feel very small indeed when we consider how easily we shun even the smallest pain. We want to complain and blame everyone for even the smallest injustice unlike Jesus who suffered in silence. We must resolve to lead better lives. Everything that happened to Jesus thus far was only a prelude to the actual act of crucifixion. This inhuman form of punishment by the Romans was intended to frighten people into submission to their rule. The crucified person would hang on the cross for days as the blood slowly left the body and the person died. It was a very cruel death. Because he had been so severely maltreated beforehand, Jesus died in only a matter of hours instead of days. The cross had been previously predrilled to make the nails easier to hammer home. The sound of the hammer echoed around the hill as Jesus suffered this further pain in his hands. The hands that blessed people with the blessing of God. The hands that healed eyes, ears, and tongues was now prevented from doing further good. The gates of hell roared with glee as the heavens were silent. The feet of Jesus were likewise nailed to the cross. The feet that brought comfort to everyone and hastened to do good were now immobilized. The groans of pain that were uttered by Jesus were but a reflection of the total agony felt by Jesus which pervaded his entire body and soul. Remember that Jesus had the perfect integrity of body and soul. Every physical and verbal act by others toward Jesus was felt by Jesus throughout his entire body and soul. A pain which we cannot understand as we do not have this gift of preternatural integrity. This love of Jesus goes beyond our level of understanding. It should be ever recalled by us so that we can at least strive to do the will of God who loves us so much. The cross of Jesus is raised to fit in the earthen hole prepared for it and with a mighty thud, the cross slides into place shaking the body of Jesus causing him further pain. Pain from the previous injuries done to Jesus may have numbed him somewhat, but now there goes through his entire body this new pain. When the suffering that we may endure at times continues on and on, we need to consider what sufferings Jesus bore for us. Let us learn from Jesus how to bear our sufferings and pains and offer it up to the suffering Jesus for the sinners that Jesus died for. Jesus now hangs, rather impaled with nails, on the wood of a cross between two criminals on a hill for all to see. The wooden sign on the cross says the King of the Jews. Though meant by the Romans to mock the Jews, it was really true. Jesus is King of the Jews and also King of us. Just as a wooden tree bore the fruit of an apple that resulted in the future sufferings of the human race, now the fruit of a suffering Divine Human will result in the future life and happiness of a multitude of humans who accept Jesus as their God. Jesus now enters the final act of redemption, his death on the cross. Racked with pain throughout his entire body, Jesus looks out at those people assembled around the cross. The Jewish leaders with their mob of followers are jeering at him and insulting him in every way imaginable. They cry out: Come down! Save yourself! He saved others, he can't save himself! If you are God's son come down from the cross and we will believe! The reply of Jesus is: "Father, forgive them, they know not what they do." Yes, indeed! If Jesus came down now, then all his sufferings would have been in vain. The human race can only be released from the power of Satan and everlasting death by the death of Jesus. Are we able to forgive those that treat us badly in the same manner that Jesus did? Our eternal salvation may depend upon it. Crucified on each side of Jesus were two criminals of the worst sort. One criminal says that if you are the Messiah then save yourself and us. The other criminal rebukes him and points out that they have been justly condemned, but that Jesus was entirely innocent. He doesn't ask to be saved, but only to be remembered when Jesus enters his kingdom. What a great act of faith. He actually believes that Jesus is going to heaven in spite of all that he sees. Jesus tells him: "Amen, I say to you, today you will be with me in Paradise." If you are ever at a point when everything seems hopeless, remember this moment. A worthless criminal with a life of crime including who knows how many killings is the first one to enter heaven because of his sincere act of repentance and faith in Jesus. A person needs only to be sincerely sorry for his past sins, resolve to sin no more, and do whatever penance is necessary and make an act of faith in Jesus. Then all is forgiven. Near the cross of Jesus among a few women is the mother of Jesus and the Apostle John. Jesus tells his mother: "Woman, behold your son." He tells John: "Behold your mother." Jesus in the midst of his sufferings remembers that his mother Mary needs someone to look after her, so he places her in the care of John. However, there is more to this than it seems. Mary is called woman rather than mother and John is not really her son. The reality is that Mary is appointed to be the true spiritual mother of all mankind. She is there ready to help us whenever we call on her. There are many times in our life when it seems like God has abandoned us. When a person is in extreme pain or lying at the hour of death, it seems like everything is lost for that person and that God has abandoned him. Does God really know what it is like? Jesus on the cross has only his human nature as his divine nature is in heaven. So Jesus shows that he too knows what true abandonment is like as he cries out: "My God, my God, why have you forsaken me?" Yes, Jesus feels the true sense of being alone, where there is nothing but the deep darkness of despair. Nearing the end of his life, Jesus cries out: "I thirst." The empty dry feeling that Jesus must have felt at this moment is understandable. His mouth was so dry that it is a wonder that he could even speak any words. The thirst of Jesus goes deeper than his earthly thirst for someting to drink. The real hunger and thirst that Jesus has is to save souls from hell and the clutches of the devil. Why else would Jesus suffer so much when he could have so easily avoided it. We speak so easily of love and we use this word so freely for so many things and some of them very mundane. This though is real love. This is manly love. This is a love offering the best of everything to the one that is loved and for all eternity. No one can make you a better offer. Finally at the end, Jesus says: "It is finished." Jesus has done everything he could possibly do to save the human race that together with the Father he created. As the second Person of the Blessed Trinity, Jesus had become one of us through the Blessed Virgin Mary. Now he would be able to offer a sacrifice that would satisfy the Divine Justice. He lived exactly like one of us and that in extreme poverty. He gathered his disciples around him who would be able to form his Church when he left them. He taught them and the Jewish people whom God had personally selected to be the group that would bring salvation to the human race. His passion was over, it was truly finished. Now, there was only one thing left for Jesus to do. He prayed: "Father, into your hands I commend my spirit." Then Jesus died. The sins of the entire human race were atoned for and all that remained for each man and woman was to embrace God and accept the way of life that God had originally intended. The gates of heaven were open but not on man's terms, but on God's. These last words of Jesus are so beautiful. They are the words that we need to use. We need to always commend ourselves to God. Place yourself in the hands of God and you will never have anything to worry about. Just remember the sacrifice that Jesus went through. Even after death, the body of Jesus had to suffer another wound. A soldier thrust his lance into the heart of Jesus and blood and water flowed out. This action would become the beginning of the Church of God. The blood symbolized the Eucharist which Jesus said one needs to attain everlasting life and the water symbolized Baptism which Jesus gave us so that we could be reborn. The Apostles would use these and other sacraments to bring people into God's kingdom. Jesus is now taken down lovingly from the cross by his friends and placed into the arms of his loving mother, Mary. How sorrowful Mary must have been to now see firsthand the terrible outrages that were worked on her son as she lovingly removed the thorns and wiped his face and body. Jesus is then placed in a tomb built out of rock. Consider now the state of affairs that the apostles and disciples of Jesus faced. Even though they had been warned many times by Jesus that this would happen, they did not anticipate the event. They were completely demoralized. They felt that their life was over. All the dreams that they had about an earthly Messianic kingdom, where all would be heavenly, were shattered. There was nothing left for them. The women planned to go to the tomb Sunday and properly prepare the body. Mary the mother of Jesus did not go because she knew what was to happen. This is a warning to us not to lose heart and assume the worst when we see and hear about terrible things happening to Catholics and Christians. Remember what Jesus said. It is not this death that one should be afraid of but the second death.

RESURRECTION

*A*nd on the first day of the week, very early in the morning, they came to the sepulcher, bringing the spices which they had prepared. And they found the stone rolled back from the sepulcher. And going in, they found not the body of the Lord Jesus. And it came to pass, as they were astonished in their mind at this, behold, two men stood by them, in shining apparel. And as they were afraid and bowed down their countenance towards the ground, they said unto them: Why seek you the living with the dead? He is not here, but is risen. Remember how he spoke unto you, when he was yet in Galilee, Saying: The Son of man must be delivered into the hands of sinful man and be crucified and the third day rise again. And they remembered his words. And going back from the sepulcher, they told all these things to the eleven and to all the rest. And it was Mary Magdalen and Joanna and Mary of James and the other women that were with them, who told these things to the apostles. And these words seemed to them as idle tales: and they did not believe them. But Peter rising up, ran to the sepulcher and, stooping down, he saw the linen cloths laid by themselves: and went away

wondering in himself at that which was come to pass.
(LK 24:1-12)

After the passion and death of Jesus on the Passover Friday, the Sabbath day began. During that day throughout Jerusalem and much of Judea all the talk among the people was about the manner and death of Jesus. The followers of Jesus were dumfounded and sad at the great tragedy that had befallen their great teacher and healer. The one they thought would be the Messiah and lead the country to freedom. Now all seemed lost. Many times in history we read of times when everything looks bleak and dark and lost. Then all of a sudden everything changes and everything is better than ever. We need to take to heart this lesson and remember it when we are in a similar situation. So long as we have our faith in Jesus we are never lost. We should note that Mary, the mother of Jesus, did not go to the tomb with the women. Mary knew that Jesus would rise from the dead. She surely had listened carefully to Jesus and had clearly understood what had escaped all the rest. We can also be sure that Jesus appeared to Mary and consoled her for her sufferings as well as his. Mary is always in the background as the main focus must always be on Jesus. The first recorded meeting of Jesus is with Mary Magdalen. Mary had been so focused on her own sorrow and unhappiness that she missed the angel's message. She was still looking for the dead Jesus. It was only when Jesus spoke her name that she realized that it was Jesus alive and speaking to her. Many times in our own life we focus on ourselves too much and miss the greater picture. This is especially in times of great events in our lives that make us very unhappy and we then wish to strike out and find a culprit when there is none. When Peter and John ran to the tomb and looked in, they see nothing but empty cloths and no Jesus. Note that there was no angel to give them the message he gave the women. Both men went back to town wondering what this meant. The horror of the passion of Jesus had so transfixed them that they still could not realize that Jesus had risen and was alive. This is understandable considering the times and the horrible death that Jesus had endured. Two of Jesus's disciples, Luke and Cleophas, listened to the stories of the empty tomb and the tale that the women told of Jesus having risen from the dead. They did not know what to make of it. They went on a short journey to a nearby town discussing all the way the recent events that had happened. Jesus joined them although they did not recognize him. Could it be that it was because of their lack of belief in the women's story? Jesus asked them what recent events were they talking about.. They told him about all that had happened and of their inability to make sense of any of it. Then Jesus proceeded to point out in the scriptures starting with Moses all that was foretold of him. Their hearts were full of joy as Jesus explained everything to them. So they asked Jesus to join them at the inn. When Jesus broke the bread, they then recognized him and Jesus disappeared. They rushed back to Jerusalem to tell the others. When they told them that they had seen Jesus, they were told in turn that Jesus had appeared to Peter. The appearance of Jesus to Peter is not recorded in the Gospels, but we can imagine how it must have happened. Peter would have certainly been overcome with joy at seeing the master alive once more. Then he would have knelt down and begged forgiveness for the times that he had denied Jesus. Forgiving Peter, Jesus would then have given him some instructions. Probably the most important was the need for Peter to strengthen the others in the days to come. There are times when we deny Jesus by our actions and maybe even by our words. Remember that there is always forgiveness. The denier of Jesus was forgiven. Later in the week when the Apostles were together in the upper room, then suddenly Jesus, Himself, appears. The Apostles and disciples are terrified and they think that they have seen a ghost. Jesus tells them to feel his flesh and to touch him so as to show that it is really him. He asks for something to eat and eats some fish. After their initial reaction, the disciples are elated. Jesus scolds them for not believing the women and the others who told of his appearances. It is important that the Apostles understand that Jesus is the Messiah spoken of in the scriptures. So Jesus explains to them how the scriptures foretold his appearance and his sufferings and death. It had to be clear to the Apostles, so that they could teach others, especially the Jews. Then Jesus makes clear to them what his mission is and how the Apostles and the disciples were to undergo their mission. His mission was not to bring an earthly kingdom in being, but rather to bring forgiveness of sins. They were the witnesses that Jesus was the Messiah and that he had conquered death and the devil. They were to go forward to preach this to all the nations as the fruits of Christ's redemption were for everyone not just the Jews. At this time Jesus gave the power to forgive sins to the Apostles. He breathed on them and gave them the Holy Spirit. This then was the beginning of the Catholic Church. There was still more to be done which would come later on. Now Thomas, one of the twelve Apostles, was not present when this event happened. The other Apostles told him about the appearance of Jesus and all that had happened. However, Thomas was unconvinced. Thomas said that he would not believe unless he could see the nail holes in the hands of Jesus and place his fingers in them and put his hand in the side of Jesus. Thomas must have seen the horrific figure of Jesus after his death and he just could not accept that anyone could be alive, even Jesus. It is so easy to fault Thomas for being so disbelieving. We have the evidence of history on our side. We like to believe that we would not have been so disbelieving like Thomas. Yet the truth of the matter is that we would have been just like Thomas if not more so. When it comes to other matters we are so easily willing to accept what others tell us, but when it comes to religious matters we want proof. The words of eyewitnesses are not enough for us. Let us pray that we will be more open to the teachings of Holy Mother Church which comes to us directly from the Apostles and has the mark of 20 centuries of miracles and witnesses of so many holy Saints. Thomas doubts that the resurrection of Jesus is possible and he thinks that the others are grasping at straws. Eight days later, Thomas is present with all the other Apostles in the upper room when Jesus suddenly appears again in the room although the doors were closed. Jesus goes directly to Thomas and tells him to place his fingers in the nail holes and his hand in his side and be believing. Thomas does this and immediately falls to the ground in adoration and pronounces those beautiful words: "My Lord and My God". Yes, Thomas not only believes that Jesus is alive, but that he is God. Jesus then speaks the words that are meant for all of us: "Because thou hast seen me, Thomas, thou hast believed: blessed are they that have not seen and have believed". It is true that we have not seen Jesus physically, but we know that he is present to us when we have had our sins forgiven and we have resolved to lead the life that Jesus has marked out for us. He is even more present to us when we receive him in the Eucharist. We show that we believe in Jesus when we receive Jesus, present in the Eucharistic Host, in Holy Communion. At that moment Jesus is present within us just as he was to Thomas. Do we understand this mystery or how it can be? No! But we accept it because we believe in the eyewitnesses who passed this on to us in the Church. There is no record in scriptures of anyone else whom Jesus may have appeared to at this time, but this does not necessarily mean that other appearances did not occur. The apostles and disciples leave Jerusalem and go to Galilee as Jesus had instructed them. The resurrection of Jesus is the central tenet of our faith. It is the most glorious happening in all of history. The suffering and death of Jesus conquered sin and death. It wiped out all of mankind's guilt. However, without Jesus rising from the dead, all this would be meaningless. For us the greater question is, will this act of Jesus be meaningless for us. It will unless we live the life that Jesus has laid out for us. The great tragedy would be if we failed to follow Jesus and wound up in hell. Then this great act of Jesus for us would have been in vain. It is important to keep the events of the Passion and Death of Jesus together with his Resurrection. Our belief is based not only on our faith in God, but also our reason shows us that the historical events that our faith is based on are true. There are the biblical prophecies about a savior or messiah and the suffering servant of Yahweh. There are the eyewitnesses who saw the events of the Gospels. And there are the events that happened in the Catholic Church over the centuries where Jesus or one of the saints has appeared to various persons. Faith and reason go together. Let us pray that the Holy Spirit will lead and guide us to our ultimate happiness with Jesus in heaven.

ASCENSION

A *nd he said to them: Thus it is written, and thus it behoved Christ to suffer and to rise again from the dead, the third day: And that penance and remission of sins should be preached in his name, unto all nations, beginning at Jerusalem. And you are witnesses of these things. And I send the promise of my Father upon you: but stay you in the city till you be endued with power from on high. And he led them out as far as Bethania: and lifting up his hands, he blessed them. And it came to pass, whilst he blessed them, he departed from them and was carried up to heaven. And they adoring went back into Jerusalem with great joy. And they were always in the temple, praising and blessing God. Amen. (LK 24: 46-53)*

Jesus appeared to the disciples for forty days after his resurrection showing himself so that they would know that he was alive and had arisen. Also he spoke about the kingdom of God and reiterated what he had said so many times during his three years on earth. After Jesus had appeared to the Apostles in Jerusalem several times, they went to Galilee as he had requested them to do. We can only guess at the reason that Jesus wanted them there. Perhaps they needed to get away from Jerusalem where the tragic events of last week had happened or perhaps Jesus knew that they would be more comfortable in Galilee. While they were waiting for Jesus to show himself, Peter decided to go fishing and the fishermen Apostles joined him and they went out in several boats. Fishing all night, they caught nothing. A man standing on the shore asked how they were doing and they replied that they had caught nothing. He said cast your net on the other side. When they did this, they caught an enormous amount of fish. John recognized that this sort of event had happened before with Jesus. He told Peter that it is the Lord. Peter then jumped into the water and came to Jesus. On the shore, Jesus had several cooked fish and bread for the Apostles to eat. There was no doubt in their mind now that it was Jesus. They knew it was him. Here we see Jesus acting the role of servant even after his resurrection. Once again Jesus emphasizes the need for us to serve our fellow man rather than to look to be served. We see also that all fear of the Jewish authorities was not present and the Apostles were more at home again with the Lord. Sitting by the lake, Jesus could teach once again the message that the Apostles were to deliver as Jesus would leave them very soon. It is only little by little that Jesus could get the Apostles away from the notion of an earthly Messiah. In other words they needed to concentrate on doing what Jesus had taught them. When we want to do something out of the ordinary, then we need to pray that what we would be doing does not go against the will of God. There are many things which seem so right to us, but they really aren't.

Sometimes we are blinded by our own wishes and don't realize that we would be going against the wishes of God. So we need to be careful and pray always. And we are very fortunate that we have the Catholic Church to look to for guidance. And if there seems to be conflicting opinions in the Church then we must look to the Pope. The Pope cannot err in matters of faith and morals because Jesus has promised to be with him till the end of time. How many times have we looked forward to something only to be disappointed because things didn't turn out the way we wanted. This is what happened to the Apostles but now they were so happy that their Jesus was alive again. But their mission would result in martyrdom for all of them except John. There would not be for them an earthly kingdom, but rather a glorious life after death in the kingdom of Heaven when everything will be made new. The operative word here is trust or faith. We need to trust Jesus and have faith in him that no matter what happens here on earth, things will turn out better than we could ever have imagined. It was at this time that Jesus placed Peter at head of his Church. Three times Jesus asked Peter if he loved him. Three times Peter said that he did. And Jesus told Peter to feed his lambs and his sheep. In other words, Jesus was entrusting the care of his Church into Peter's hands. It would be Peter who would take the place of Jesus here on earth and lead his people in prayerful worship. It would be Peter that the faithful Christians would look to for the true teachings of Jesus. Peter along with the Apostles would proclaim the Gospel or good news of salvation. It is only now that the Apostles are told to baptize in the name of the Father and the Son and the Holy Spirit. This is the baptism that erases not only original sin but all personal sin. Now that

Jesus has suffered and died for our sins, Baptism takes on a new meaning when it is done in the name of the Father, the Son, and the Holy Spirit. How fortunate are those who accept Jesus Christ as their savior and are born anew in the waters of Baptism. Jesus repeats the teachings that he had given so many times during the last three years. We can be sure that he repeated his basic message of love of God and love of neighbor. From the first commandment to love God with our whole heart and soul and body flows all the other commandments including the love of neighbor. While the Apostles and disciples of Jesus had more courage and were now full of hope, they were still a long way from being the soldiers of Christ that would be needed in the days to come. Jesus promised to send them the Spirit of truth, that is, the Holy Spirit. It would be this Spirit that would enable them to be more open and courageous about their faith in God and Jesus their Savior. This is a good moment to pause and think about what all this means to me personally. All of this is a preparation for the ascending of Jesus into heaven. The words of Jesus at the Last Supper about leaving them now made sense to the Apostles. Jesus would go to his heavenly Father. But for us Jesus is not some God in a far away heaven. He is with us here and now every day. So long as we have not severed our friendship with God by committing a mortal sin then we are in a state of grace and Jesus can dwell within us just as he did during the maternity of Mary. When we receive the Body and Blood of Jesus in Holy Communion he dwells within us body, blood, soul, and divinity. For the brief minutes that Jesus is within us we can talk to him about our problems, ask for his help, thank him for all he has done for us in the past, or adore him because he is

God. As we think about the coming Ascension of Jesus into heaven, we should think about the day that we will die and our soul will ascend into judgment before Jesus. Are we ready? Death can happen at any moment. When we prepare for a journey, we pack many things that we will need when we arrive at our destination. We also need money to travel whether by car, train, or airplane. When we die we need no money for transportation, it's free. What do we need to pack? Nothing. What will be awaiting us when we arrive will be the life that we led here on earth. It will all be there. Our good works. Our good and evil deeds. Our prayers. Remember that Jesus said that not everyone who says to him Lord, Lord will enter, but only those who do the will of his heavenly Father. Have we done the will of God? Forty days after the Resurrection, Jesus goes to the Mount of Olives with the Apostles. The Apostles ask Jesus if he is going to restore the kingdom at this time. Jesus tells them that it is not for them to know the time or when this will happen. Even at this time, the Apostles still do not realize that it is not an earthly kingdom that we are to look forward to. We have to be careful that we do not fall into this same trap. Our focus needs to remain always on God and we will see this new kingdom in the next life. He tells them to go into Jerusalem to wait for the coming of another Advocate, the Holy Spirit, who will tell them everything. Then telling them to baptize everyone in the name of the Father, and the Son, and the Holy Spirit, he ascended into heaven where he dwells with the Father. Jesus would seem to have left the Apostles alone to fend for themselves. This, of course, is not the case. The relationship between mankind and God is unique. Even though God is to be adored because he is the Creator and nothing would exist without him, he created the human race to be in a covenant relationship with him. This relationship as Jesus taught us is to make us sharers in the Divine Nature of God as adopted sons of God. In a sense this implies a partnership with God. Jesus has accomplished all the important and necessary work through his passion and death and resurrection. The task for those who accept Jesus, hence God, is to bring many others to join in accepting Jesus. We can do this by our actions, our prayers, and by teaching all that Jesus has taught us by his words and actions. So, it is not necessary for Jesus to be physically present with us although he has done this sacramentally in the Eucharist. We now can have no fear here on earth before we die, because we know that we have in heaven a person like us in the humanity of Jesus who while also being God is able to be our advocate and mediator with God the Father. When judgment day comes and we stand before the judgment seat of God, our judge will be our good friend, Jesus. Therefore we have nothing to be afraid of so long as we remain faithful to God. And those moments when we sinned and went astray will be forgotten as if they never existed when we confessed our faults, expressed our sorrow for offending God, and resolved never to ever do these sins again. So we should be happy and joyful, knowing that a wonderful life awaits us in the next world. In this world we need to march ahead with head held high no matter what evil, pains, or sorrows happens to us. Jesus is waiting to welcome us into his heavenly home as his guest.

PENTECOST

A *nd when the days of the Pentecost were accomplished, they were all together in one place. And suddenly there came a sound from heaven, as of a mighty wind coming: and it filled the whole house where they were sitting. And there appeared to them parted tongues, as it were of fire: and it sat upon every one of them. And they were all filled with the Holy Ghost: and they began to speak with divers tongues, according as the Holy Ghost gave them to speak. (Ac 2: 1-4)*

After the ascension ot Jesus into heaven, the Apostles and the disciples of Jesus returned to Jerusalem to the upper room where they remained in prayer for ten days. Mary, the mother of Jesus, was with them as well as many women. They were all praying for the coming of the Advocate that Jesus had promised would come, the Holy Spirit. Also, they chose a successor to Judas Iscariot, the traitor, who had betrayed Jesus. The lot fell on Matthias who was numbered as one of the twelve. Even though Jesus had promised to send the Holy Spirit, it was necessary for everyone to pray earnestly to God for this to happen. Once again we see how important it is to pray. The Apostles could have laid back and waited for the promised Holy Spirit. However, they knew it was very necessary for them to pray for the coming of the Holy Spirit. The lesson for us is that prayer is not only important, but that it is vital for us Christians to be very persevering in prayer if we expect to receive what we are praying for. The more we pray, the better chance we have for a prompt answer to our prayers. It should also be noted that the Apostles took time out from prayer to take care of other important matters such as the successor to Judas. We cannot completely ignore everything in order to pray. A proper perspective is needed to do the necessary tasks while giving prayer an important part of our life. Remember that the mother of Jesus, Mary, was also there praying with the women for this coming of the Holy Spirit on the Apostles. Thus the importance of the community united in a single purpose praying together. The coming of the Holy Spirit was marked by a mighty wind and then tongues of fire over the Apostles. They had received the Holy Spirit in a remarkable manner so that there would be no mistake about what was occurring. The mighty wind reminds us that God is coming. The tongues of fire remind us that the knowledge given to the Apostles is to be given to others. The fire reminds us that this is not ordinary knowledge, but the knowledge of God destined to set one on fire with the love of God. This great outpouring of the Holy Spirit results in the Apostles being filled with courage, knowledge of Jesus and God, and the strong fearless desire to impart this teaching of Jesus to others. They were all aflame with the love of God. One can ask why we are not aflame with the same longing as we have received this same Holy Spirit when we were baptized and confirmed in the Church. I believe that the answer is that these men were fishermen and they had to go out and confront a hostile world of their own countrymen and the pagans. They also spent eight days praying. They were to meet many hardships including scorn and torture and finally in every case a cruel death. They also had the task of setting up the foundation for the Catholic Church. What these men accomplished is truly amazing. Yet, it is this same Holy Spirit that we have received to strengthen us in our faith and should be our guiding light in our earthly journey here on earth. Receiving the Holy Spirit is not enough. We must use the strength that the Spirit gives us to motivate ourselves for our love of God and his Church. We need to resolve to learn more about our faith which after all is knowledge of Jesus and the key to understand what God wants of us in the life we are leading in this place and at this time in history. Filled with the Holy Spirit, Peter and the Apostles go outside and preach to the crowds of Jews gathered there. They are a mixture of people from all over the known world at that time. They are astonished to hear these Galileans speaking to them in their native language. The teachings of Peter and the Apostles about Jesus to the multitude was so effective that the people wanted to know what they should do. Peter told them to do penance, be baptized in the name of Jesus Christ for the remission of their sins. Then you shall receive the gift of the Holy Spirit. Peter's words remind us that our receiving of the Holy Spirit is a gift. It is not enough to sit back and let the Holy Spirit work in us. We must do our part as Jesus had said that not everyone who says Lord, Lord, will enter the kingdom of heaven, but only the one who does the will of his Father. We must be active in prayer, works of mercy and the funding of charities. This will fulfill our mission to help others both spiritually and physically especially the poor. What can happen when we are filled with the Holy Spirit is demonstrated by the Apostles on the first Pentecost when 3,000 souls were baptized and added to the Church. Further more we are told that the newly baptized were persevering in the doctrine of the Apostles. In other words they accepted fully the teachings of Jesus as given to them by the Church. They were learning what it means to be a Christian. The newly converted could now participate in Holy Communion. The Body and Blood of Jesus was now their spiritual nourishment. And they were persevering in prayer. Further, they held everything in common, so that no one had possessions of his or her own. Those who were in need were taken care of by those who had plenty. They sold their possessions and gave the money to the poor. The community was united as one. This is the way each Church community should be like. While it is not necessary to live together and sell all our possessions, we need to use our surplus to help others and at times make sacrifices for the sake of Christ who gave his all for us. The Bible tells of many other events that happened after this coming of the Holy Spirit. While the Holy Spirit had worked many times in the Old Testament, it is nothing like the outpouring of the Holy Spirit after Pentecost. The history of the Catholic Church is full of the miracles worked by various Saints throughout the centuries that have been documented. This doesn't take into account the many cases of those that were not written about. Each time a sacrament is conferred on a person by the Church, that person receives a grace from the Holy Spirit which is intended to help him or her lead a life of Christ in conformity with the state in life that that person has chosen. We usually don't feel different or experience anything differently, but we have received what we need to advance in the spiritual life according to our needs. The Holy Spirit helps us focus on the really important matters in life. Jesus emphasized the importance of persevering in prayer. The Holy Spirit help us to accomplish that. Saul was persecuting the early Christians and was converted by an action of Jesus. This conversion surely took place because of the prayers of the early Christian communities who had been filled with the Holy Spirit. As a result, Saul became Paul, one of the great Apostles second only to Peter. Paul filled with the Holy Spirit went on to convert people all over the Mediterranean countries. He endured beatings, ship wrecks, hunger, and many other dangers in his quest to convert everyone to Christ. Yet, he acknowledged that what he did was nothing because of the great harm he had done earlier to the Church. He willingly gave his life for Christ. That is what it means to be a Christian. We should be asking ourselves the question as to how we can use this gift of the Holy Spirit that we have all received in Baptism and all the other sacraments. Some thoughts from St. Symeon called the New Theologian who wrote in the tenth century. "Those who are baptized must be aware of the presence of the Holy Spirit. Christian life is an intimate and personal communion with God. Divine grace illumines the believer's heart and leads him to the mystical vision of the Lord. True knowledge of God stems from a journey of interior purification which begins with conversion of heart, thanks to the strength of faith and love. It then passes through profound repentance and sincere sorrow for one's sins and then arrives at union with Christ, source of joy and peace." For St. Symeon, such an experience of divine grace is not an exceptional gift for some mystics, but the fruit of Baptism in the life of every seriously committed faithful person. These words of St. Symeon should inspire hope in us if we remember that the operative word is seriously committed faithful. Are we seriously committed to our faith? Are we seriously committed to Jesus? Are we seriously committed to the Catholic Church founded by Christ? If not then we need to work on arriving at this union with Christ. If we are not in mortal sin, then there is a hidden presence of God within us. God is not in some lofty heaven far away out of our sight. He is within us and we need to realize this and cooperate with the Holy Spirit to grow more aware of his presence. This holy monk, St. Symeon gives us some clues. We need a spiritual life as part of our daily life. This can consist of many different things according to our state of life such as daily Mass, daily reading of scriptures, daily prayers, and reading spiritual advice from the clergy. This monk also talks about honesty of conscience and purification. We need to purify our conscience of any personal desires and emotions and look to the teachings of the Church regarding faith and morals. If our conscience is truly formed by the teachings of Jesus eliminating any personal desires then we will have a truly honest conscience. This should lead us to having the Holy Spirit in us to guide us in all our actions. Is this going to be easy? Of course not. But remember that we were born to know, love, and serve God in this world so that we can enjoy happiness forever in heaven in the next life. Isn't it worth it?

ASSUMPTION

I will put enmities between thee and the woman, and thy seed and her seed: she shall crush thy head, and thou shalt lie in wait for her heel. (Ng 3: 15) And the angel being come in, said unto her: Hail, full of grace, the Lord is with thee: blessed art thou among women. (Lk 1: 28) Because he hath regarded the humility of his handmaid: for behold from henceforth all generations shall call me blessed. Because he that is mighty hath done great things to me: and holy is his name. (Lk 1: 48-49) And Simeon blessed them and said to Mary his mother: Behold this child is set for the fall and for the resurrection of many in Israel and for a sign which shall be contradicted. And thy own soul a sword shall pierce, that, out of many hearts thoughts may be revealed. (Lk 2: 34-35) Now there stood by the cross of Jesus, his mother and his mother's sister, Mary of Cleophas, and Mary Magdalen. When Jesus therefore had seen his mother and the disciple standing whom he loved, he saith to his mother: Woman, behold thy son. After that, he saith to the disciple: Behold thy mother. And from that hour, the disciple took her to his own. (Jn 19: 25-27)

There is not much written about the Blessed Virgin Mary in the Bible as the great emphasis had to be placed on our Lord Jesus Christ. After all, his saving act of redemption is the primary focus of our faith. We know Mary to be a very humble person. Certainly she wanted all the attention to be paid to her son. Mary is an innocent obedient and holy maiden. Her greatest role is that of one who participates in the passion of Jesus even though she is on the sidelines. We know this from the words of Simeon that a sword will pierce her soul. How can one say that? Mary was conceived without original sin in anticipation of the redemptive act of Jesus. This means she was sinless at birth. The only way that God could become incarnate within her. Also, this means that she possessed the preternatural gift of "integrity." In other word there was complete harmony within her person between her flesh and her spirit. "Integrity" means that her natural desires were under complete control of her will. Since her will was completely and utterly in love with God, she was able to be sinless. Mary was just like Adam and Eve before their fall into the original sin. While this is such a great gift, there is also a downside to it. Every negative remark or injury made to Mary or one of her loved ones or God resonated into the depths of her soul. What that means is that if someone made an unjust injurious remark, say about Jesus, this would be as if some one slapped her in the depths of her soul. If you keep this in mind, then it is much easier to imagine the terrible sufferings that Mary suffered especially in her seven sorrows. When Mary was dying, the twelve Apostles were summoned to come to her side according to one tradition. When Mary died, all were present except for Thomas. Thomas arrived after Mary had already been buried and he was insistent that they let him look on her countenance. So, the coffin was dug up and opened and behold, it was empty. They knew then that Mary had been assumed into heaven. Some theologians believe that Mary was only in a deep sleep. I believe that she undoubtedly wished to experience death just as her Lord and Savior did. While Mary is never worshipped, the Catholic Church places her far above all the other saints. The reasoning for this is not only because she gave birth to the Son of God, but because she cooperated with Jesus in his life and death. She accepted the will of God in whatever happened to her and Joseph. She remained sinless throughout her entire life. Let us follow Mary through her life so that we can better understand her exalted status in life. At a very young age Mary was brought to the temple in Jerusalem to be raised by the women attendants. It was there that she learned to love God and vowed to be his obedient servant. Mary took a vow of virginity so that she could concentrate her whole attention and life to prayer and pleasing God. When she was told to take Joseph as her husband, she did not question the authorities, but accepted Joseph as her husband. It caused her some worry naturally because of her vow of virginity, but she was relieved to find that Joseph had taken a similar vow. None of this is in the Bible and of course you need not accept it. At this time in Jerusalem, there was talk of the imminent coming of the Messiah as foretold by the prophets. Mary prayed constantly and deeply that she would be accepted as the servant girl for the mother of the Messiah. Imagine her surprise when the angel told her that she was to give birth to the Messiah. She was further told that it was to be accomplished through the power of the Holy Spirit. Without hesitation she gave her consent. Mary made no objections. She accepted obediently and immediately with faith the will of God. Further, Mary didn't run to Joseph and say guess what happened. She kept this all to herself, trusting that God in his good time will make everything come out the way he wants. This is truly great faith in God. Who of us have a faith as great as that? Mary learns from the angel that her cousin, Elizabeth, is with child. She goes immediately to see her and her exchange of greetings with Elizabeth is one of her great joys. Of course, Joseph after a few months notices that Mary is with child. He says nothing as he does not wish to embarrass her and he privately plans to divorce her quietly. The angel comes in a dream and explains the situation. So Joseph takes her into his home. I am sure there are no other couples as loving and trusting as these two. The Roman census complicates matters for Mary as she is forced to go to Bethlehem as her time to deliver her child nears. Jesus is born in a cave as no other place is available for the couple. In spite of the hardship and surroundings, Mary is full of happiness at the birth of Jesus. There is no complaint from her lips. We should take note of this as we complain when we are just inconvenienced a little bit. The presentation of Jesus in the Jerusalem Temple brings Mary her first great sorrow when she hears that her son will not receive a warm reception when he starts his mission. Up to this time Mary would have assumed that Jesus, the Messiah, would receive a warm reception from his fellow countrymen. This news wounded her deeply. The next blow came quickly as King Herod sought to kill the infant Jesus. So, Joseph and Mary had to flee to Egypt where they lived as poor aliens in a foreign land. Mary could accept living in a foreign land with her usual acceptance of God's will, but that the death of her son was wanted by others grieved her deeply. Joseph and Mary return to Judea when it is safe and settle down in the town of Nazareth. Mary's next sorrow takes place when suddenly at the age of twelve, her Jesus is nowhere to be found. After three days of frantic search, Jesus is found in the Jerusalem Temple conversing with the Rabbis. Mary asks Jesus as to why he did this, only to be reminded that he was more than her child. Mary is seldom mentioned during the three years of Jesus's teaching mission. During the wedding feast at Cana, we learn that Jesus does indeed listen to his mother. She undoubtedly assisted Jesus and his disciples along with the other women during his teaching mission. The greatest ordeal of Mary took place during the passion and death of Jesus. It was at this time that the very real physical sword of pain and sufferings would pierce the very soul of Mary as she suffered along with Jesus. She became in essence a co-redeemer. We now need to stop and explain what we mean. Only Jesus can redeem mankind from all sin including original sin since he is both God and man. Remember what St. Paul said: "It makes me happy to suffer for you, as I am suffering now, and in my own body to do what I can to make up all that has still to be undergone by Christ for the sake of his body, the Church." (Co 1: 24) Mary, St. Paul, and each of us participate in Christ's redemption in a subordinate manner for the body of Christ, the Catholic Church. God wants us to cooperate with him to bring about the final triumph of his Church. We can do this by our words, actions, and good works. We do this to help others get to heaven, but we do this mostly by the same way Jesus did, that is, by taking up our cross daily and offering it up to the Father just as Jesus did. So, in effect when we do this we are a co-redeemer with Christ. Mary experienced four great sorrows during the passion of Jesus. Four events that pierced her heart and soul like one that no other person had ever experienced. Words cannot express the terrible sufferings that this innocent woman endured as she witnessed the terrible price that Jesus had to pay for your sins and mine. The first event during the passion took place when Mary met Jesus on the way to Calvary. Up till then, Mary suffered along with Jesus spiritually not having actually witnessed the terrible beatings that his body took. However, when she met him face to face and she could see the flesh torn, blood dripping, the crown of thorns on his head and his body barely able to walk, it was as if a sharp spear had pierced her soul. You and I cannot imagine her sufferings. Mary had scarcely recovered from this meeting, when she now saw the crucifixion of Jesus. The sound of the nails being driven into the hands and feet of Jesus echoed in the ears of Mary and she could scarcely stand as she heard the groans of her beloved Jesus. It was our sins that were hammered into the sacred flesh of Jesus. Whenever we receive any injury of any kind we need to remember what our sins did and offer up our little crosses to Jesus in reparation. A dead Jesus was laid on the lap of Mary and she gently removed the thorns and washed the wounds of her Lord. Another tremendous sorrow ripped through the body of Mary and injured her soul once again. Alas, there is no end to the sufferings of Mary. Our sins have not only caused the sufferings and death of Jesus, but we have scarred the soul of our dear mother Mary. At the burial of Jesus, Mary thought that it would have been better if she would have suffered instead of

Jesus. She could hardly bear to see Jesus laid in the tomb. Mary lingered as long as she could, the sorrow she felt at that moment was still great. Her son was dead. We killed him with our sins. While we are all co-redeemers in the true sense of the word, but in a subordinate way, Mary was the first. Because of the sufferings that she endured, she is unique and she deservedly is entitled to the title of Co-Redemtrix. The Blessed Virgin Mary is our mother and she has been blessed throughout the ages as was prophesied about her. She deserved to be assumed into heaven, body and soul, to enjoy the fruits of heaven. Mary shows and leads us the way to Heaven.

CORONATION

*A*nd Joseph also went up from Galilee, out of the city of Nazareth, into Judea, to the city of David, which is called Bethlehem: because he was of the house and family of David. To be enrolled with Mary his espoused wife, who was with child. And it came to pass that when they were there, her days were accomplished that she should be delivered. (Lk 2: 4-6) And after eight days were accomplished, that the child should be circumcised, his name was called Jesus, which was called by the angel before he was conceived in the womb. (Lk 2:21) And the wine failing, the mother of Jesus saith to him: They have no wine. And Jesus saith to her: Woman, what is that to me and to thee? My hour is not yet come. His mother saith to the waiters: Whatsoever he shall say to you, do ye. (Jn 2: 3-5) Jesus answered: My kingdom is not of this world. If my kingdom were of this world, my servants would certainly strive that I should not be delivered to the Jews: but now my kingdom is not from hence. (Jn 18: 36) When Jesus therefore had seen his mother and the disciple standing whom he loved, he saith to his mother: Woman, behold thy son. After that, he saith to *the disciple: Behold thy mother. And from that hour, the disciple took her to his own. (Jn 19: 26-27) And a great sign appeared in heaven: A woman clothed with the sun, and the moon under her feet, and on her head a crown of twelve stars. (Rv 12: 1)*

From the earliest times, Mary has been spoken of as a Queen as she was the mother of Jesus, the acknowledged King of the Universe. Mary, of course, is the Queen Mother of Jesus by right of his birth. However, she is rightly given this title because of several other factors. Mary was the only human who was sinless not only from original sin but also from personal sin. Mary participated in the passion of Jesus intimately as the sorrows she felt during the passion pierced her very soul so that she could be called Co-Redemtrix par excellence. No one else in human history has or will participate so fully and completely as Mary. We are all called to be co-redeemers, but none of us will come close to Mary. We were given a glimpse of Mary's role as an Advocate at Cana when she told Jesus that they had no wine. Notice that Mary is addressed as woman not as mother. Jesus perceives Mary as speaking as an advocate. Mary's words to the attendants show that she knows that Jesus will do something even though he warned her that his action would bring him closer to the cross. Mary has not been an inactive Queen throughout the centuries, but has been active in reminding us of the great love that God has for each and every one of us. We will meditate on some of the various visits that Mary has undertaken to help bring mankind back to God. The devil tries to confuse us with false apparitions so we will only meditate on apparitions which have met the approval of the local Bishop of the Catholic Church. In the year 1208, St. Dominic had been trying to convert the Albigensians, a French sect, that was prevalent in Southern France at that time. Their doctrine was that only the spiritual was good and that everything material was evil. The Blessed Virgin Mary appeared to him and told him to preach the rosary which contained the Angelic Salutation and the Our Father prayer from the Bible. St. Dominic did so and the Albigensians were for the most part converted. We learn from this the powerful graces that flow from the recitation of the rosary. In 1251 Mary appeared to St. Simon Stock and told him that those who wore a special brown scapular would receive special graces. Of course wearing this scapular in itself means nothing unless the person wearing it is in a state of grace and striving to live a life full of prayer and love for God. Mary was given the title of Our Lady of Mount Carmel as a result of this event. The first of three major apparitions took place in 1531 in Aztec Mexico. The civil administrators treated the Aztecs with cruelty and harshness. The missionaries insisted that they be treated with respect. Bishop Zumarraga smuggled out a message in a hollowed out crucifix that resulted in the Spanish Emperor replacing the Governor, but this took a long while to take effect. Meanwhile the Aztecs and the other tribes took to arms against the Spanish. The Bishop sensed a general insurrection was imminent and begged Our Lady to intervene. He secretly asked that Mary send him some Castilian roses as a sign that his prayer had been heard. Castilian roses were unknown in Mexico. Few conversions to the faith took place as the natives clung to their old gods. Juan Diego, a native convert, was met by the Blessed Virgin Mary and told to tell the Bishop to have a temple built on Tepeyac hill. The Bishop listened and finally asked Juan Diego to have the Lady give him a sign. Later when met by Our Lady, she told Juan to climb the hill and pick the flowers and take them to the Bishop. This took place in December when nothing was growing. Juan Diego did as Mary told him and when he opened his cloak, the flowers including Castilian roses all fell out. But what was amazing was that there on the cloak of Juan Diego was an image of Mary. This image stands today in a magnificent Basilica in Mexico City and the image resulted in the conversion of thousands of natives. Mary as the advocate for the Bishop received the graces from God to answer the prayers of the Bishop far beyond his wildest dreams. In the year 1571, a large Muslim fleet was ready to invade Italy and a smaller Christian fleet went to meet them. On October 7 the two fleets met and all factors favored the Muslims. Meanwhile in Rome Pope Pius V and the congregation were praying the rosary from dawn to dusk. A sudden wind change favored the Christian fleet and they won the battle of Lepanto. As a result October 7 was instituted as the Feast of the Holy Rosary. In 1830 the Blessed Virgin appeared to a nun Catherine Laboure at the Rue du Bac in Paris, France. She asked that a medal be made with the inscription: "O Mary, conceived without sin, pray for us who have recourse to you." The medal included an image of Mary showing rays coming from her hands. These rays Mary told her were graces to be granted to those who wear the medal. She foretold terrible sufferings that were to take place in France in the future. The medal brought about so many cures that it became known as the Miraculous Medal. On September, 1846 the only appearance of Mary crying took place in a mountain village of La Salette in the French Alps in south-eastern France. She appeared to a 11 year old boy, Maximin Garaud, and a 14 year old girl, Melanie Calvat. She told them while crying that unless the people repented she would be forced to let go the arm of her Son because it had become so heavy. She complained she had to pray ceaselessly for them to her Son, but they still worked on Sundays and blasphemed God. Her appearance as Our Lady of La Salette teaches us many lessons about Mary. Where there is much sin even in a small village, Mary is praying and trying to mediate with her son to lessen punishment. She is our advocate for everyone. Without our repentance there is a limit to the patience of God. She shows us the importance of Mass on Sundays and the need to rest from work on Sunday. She tells us of the importance of not taking the name of God in vain. Mary is crying not as a symbol, but because she loves us so much. Pope Pius IX proclaimed the dogma of the Immaculate Conception in 1854. This dogma proclaimed that Mary was from the moment of her conception free from Original Sin. This sinless conception of Mary had always been believed by Catholics and now it was formalized in a Dogma. In 1858 in the village of Lourdes, France located in the south of France, Mary appeared to a 14 year old girl, Bernadette Soubirous for 18 times. Mary asked that a shrine be built and that people come in processions. On the last day, Mary revealed her name as the Immaculate Conception. The site of the apparitions was an old rubbish dump next to a grotto. Bernadette dug a hole and uncovered a spring. The waters from this spring have produced many amazing miracles. A room at the shrine houses documented evidence on almost 100 of them. Mary is known as Our Lady of Lourdes. The shrine and grotto where the apparitions took place now house several large churches, baths, Lourdes water fountains, and other religious structures. It is the most visited shrine in the Catholic world. People come and bathe in the waters, hear Mass in the churches, pray the Stations of the Cross, confess their sins, and at night there is a beautiful candlelight procession on the grounds with everyone praying the rosary aloud in their own language. We can see from this how Mary is working to help build up the Body of Christ with the help of the faithful and bestowing graces where needed. Her most powerful weapon is the rosary. Who would be foolish enough not to take advantage of such a powerful weapon. The most revealing apparition for our times occurred in 1917 in the rural countryside of Portugal near the town of Fatima. It involved three children, Lucia, Francisco, and Jacinta. During this same period of time, World War I was being fought mainly in Europe where thousands of young men were being slaughtered on the battle fields. In 1916, the angel of Portugal appeared to the three children while they were tending their sheep in the fields near Fatima, announcing himself as the Angel of Peace. He appeared three times and asked them to pray with him. He taught several prayers and urged them to pray and offer sacrifice to God for sins committed. On the third visit he gave them Holy Communion. In 1917 the Blessed Virgin Mary appeared to the three children under the title of Our Lady of the Rosary. Mary asked them to offer themselves to God along with the sufferings they will receive in atonement for the sins committed and for the conversion of sinners. She asked them to say the rosary for peace in the world and for the end of the war. After telling them that they would eventually go to heaven, she showed them hell. Mary said to save souls, God wants to establish devotion to her Immaculate Heart. If so, many souls will be saved. If men do not stop offending God, a more and terrible war will begin during the pontificate of Pope Pius XI. To prevent this, she asked that Russia be consecrated to her Immaculate Heart and that people partake of Communions of reparation on the first Saturday of every month for the atonement of the sins of the world. On the sixth and last apparition on the 13th of October, after two days of soaking rain, Mary appeared to the children. Mary said that she is the Lady of the Rosary and asked that the rosary be prayed every day and that a chapel be built at Fatima. Mary teaches us that we need to prepare ourselves by prayer, the Eucharist, and sacrifices. We can see that she is our most glorious advocate and mediator with God. We all have the role to act as redeemers, advocates, and mediators, but in a far lessor sense than Mary. We do this as St. Paul says to build up the Body of Christ.

CPSIA information can be obtained
at www.ICGtesting.com
Printed in the USA
FSHW010528010620
70774FS